HOW TO IMPROVE YOUR SOCIAL SKILLS

HOW TO IMPROVE YOUR SOCIAL SKILLS

Practical Exercises and Techniques for the Socially Challenged

DR. THOMAS LUCKING, PHD, LMFT

ROCKRIDGE PRESS

For general information on our other products and services or to obtain technical support, please contact our Customer Care Department within the United States at (866) 744-2665, or outside the United States at (510) 253-0500.

Rockridge Press publishes its books in a variety of electronic and print formats. Some content that appears in print may not be available in electronic books, and vice versa.

Interior and Cover Designer: Diana Haas
Art Producer: Tom Hood
Editor: Shannon Criss
Photography Irochka_T/iStock, cover; interior photograph mikdam/iStock.

ISBN: Print 978-1-64739-644-2 | eBook 978-1-64739-645-9
R0

This book is dedicated to those who struggle
with social interactions. I am humbled by
and grateful to my patients who have vulnerably
shared their journey and allowed our work to be a
catalyst for transformation for themselves
and future generations.

CONTENTS

INTRODUCTION

My name is Dr. Thomas Lucking, and I am the founder of Silicon Valley Therapy, where I serve as the clinical director. We are a health care group practice that offers psychological and coaching services to clients in the San Francisco Bay Area and beyond. It is from this vantage point that I look out upon a world of seven billion people trying to relate to one another, the world they inhabit, and their psychospiritual selves.

My professional career began after obtaining an undergraduate degree in computer science, and then a follow-up career as a software engineer. I was attracted to digital technology because of its interactive nature. Computers are predictable; they do what you tell them to do (not always what you want them to do). Their language is pure logic; they do not emit emotions. In fact, it was only my emotions that needed to be managed when the computer didn't do what I wanted.

At Silicon Valley Therapy, we are immersed in relationships every day: from individuals struggling with loneliness, to couples trying to make sense of a wounded relationship, to families dealing with alienation and resentment. The human social landscape is laden with challenges.

People are highly motivated by pain. My colleagues and I don't typically meet many of our clients until their symptoms have devolved to a level of suffering that impedes their daily functioning and well-being. This is unfortunate because the longer one waits with a problem, the more difficult it is to turn it around.

When assessing symptoms during a new client intake, relationships of one kind or another are always involved. The stress that is created from a lack of healthy social nurturing creates downstream psychological and physical health problems. The Holmes and Rahe Stress Scale assigns points for life stressors and then presents the probability that a given stressor will lead to physical illness. Some research reports that 70 percent of people in hospitals are there because of chronic stress.

Relationships are a big deal. They make life worth living. The British writer and theologian C. S. Lewis believed that friendships were like philosophy and art. Neither are domains of human achievement, but they do increase the value of surviving. What's more important: to be financially independent or to be loved? Why is there no direct correlation between wealth and happiness?

Before approaching the information shared in the following pages, consider the following questions: How is the health of your relationships? Do you have friends outside of your immediate family? Are you a good communicator? What is your strategy for managing disagreements and conflict? Are you transparent with your emotions in your relationships? Do you hold grudges and resentment with anyone?

PART I

THE FOUNDATION OF SOCIAL SKILLS

Why are social skills important, desired, and sought after? The short answer is because people are wired to be social. We are naturally curious about other people and have a desire to connect with them. Our values, core beliefs, and identities are formed out of our connection with other people and with groups that have identities of their own. It's almost as if our solitary self is handicapped and we need others to move us closer to wholeness, which enables us to make sense of ourselves and the world around us. However, to form these desired connections, we need social skills. But what exactly are social skills? Part 1 of this book will define and describe these skills and discuss the challenges that make it difficult to overcome social fears. These chapters will also provide guidelines that will help you identify areas where you struggle with social interactions as well as questions and prompts that will help you set goals for success as you move forward with your social skills journey.

CHAPTER 1

THE PROCESS

Social skills are necessary for higher levels of well-being. Positive psychology presents the necessary components of well-being, and healthy relationships are among them. In contrast to relationships, another component of well-being is personal achievement. Our well-being improves through achievements such as solving a problem, winning an award, closing a deal, or reaching a life goal. Relationships are different from personal achievement in that they don't always have a goal. That is to say, relationships feed our social needs in a way that doesn't always produce a measurable outcome. If one is to reach a high level of well-being or to flourish, all areas of well-being must be addressed.

While our world needs problem solvers, that's not enough. Despite humanity's highly skilled problem-solving capabilities, our global human community has not solved many problems that are rooted in relationships. From global social problems that remain unsolved due to political failures to personal problems that are not solved due to communication failures, something is missing. Problem solving focuses on content and a dogged pursuit of answers. A solitary human can solve but so much on their own. The more difficult problems in life require collaboration. Within a process of prosocial collaboration, amazing things happen. Yet for this process to occur, social skills are needed.

Could our unsolved social, relational, and personal problems be caused by a lack of social skills? Would our level of flourishing increase if we added highly effective social skills to our problem-solving abilities? What would our world and our lives look like without violent conflict, offensive communication, and indifference toward people living on the margins of society? Our world has no shortage of big problems, but change starts with you; it begins with you being part of the solution.

This change doesn't require you to be completely selfless because the payoff for you is big as well. You may experience intimacy and connection in ways you never knew were possible. Imagine getting flooded with the relationship neurochemical oxytocin on a regular basis. You know you are loved—you know you are not alone, and you know you belong. This is in stark contrast to a dominant cultural paradigm of individualism and competition. This relational path is clearly the "road less traveled," taking it might make all the difference for you, your community, and even future generations.

SOCIAL SKILLS 101

When it comes to social skills, people are not created equal. As with any talent, skill, or gift, some people are naturals, while others have to work harder at it. Why is this? Simply put, there are two reasons: brain structures and mirror neurons. Women have more bandwidth in the structure of the brain called the corpus callosum, which allows greater communication between the brain's left and right hemispheres. The right hemisphere is where feelings, intuition, and empathy reside, while the left hemisphere is where logic and language are located. Mirror neurons are mainly responsible for what are often described as feelings in "the gut." These neurons give us an emotional sense of what another person is feeling. There is a felt energetic experience during an interpersonal exchange. If you have a greater amount of mirror neurons, then social skills come easier for you. Whether social skills are easy or hard for you, remember that knowledge, practice, and perseverance can increase your abilities in this area.

Problems tend to be solved faster and more efficiently when effective social skills are behind a collaborative effort to find a solution. Employees are more motivated when they have empowering, supportive relationships with their managers. Spouses are more motivated when relational intimacy is high. Friends are more likely to contribute toward common goals when they feel included.

In the world of relationships, we say that fast is slow and slow is fast. This means that moving too fast toward a solution may result in skipping over the relational part of the process; the end result is slower progress toward a solution. On the flip side, slowing down and nurturing relationships will, in the end, actually increase the speed at which everyone moves toward a solution; this is because once a solid relational connection is made, all the people involved become much more motivated and committed to reaching a solution as quickly as possible. Without this motivation and feeling of empowerment, people drag their feet and reluctantly move forward or abandon the task altogether. Social skills are needed to nurture the relationships that help you solve problems more quickly.

BENEFITS OF SOCIAL SKILLS

Beyond problem solving, social skills have many benefits. Good social skills can create many opportunities in your life. Research by Dr. Travis Bradberry concluded that emotional intelligence, which includes social skills, is responsible for 58 percent of a person's job performance. While 90 percent of top performers have high emotional intelligence, only 20 percent of bottom performers have it.

Suppressing your emotions is not good for your mental or physical health. However, when you don't have the social skills to express your emotions in a prosocial way, you are more likely to suppress them rather than risk damaging a relationship. People who do not express their emotions in a healthy way tend to turn to less effective means of managing their feelings, such as substance abuse. They are also more likely to experience anxiety, stress, and depression.

Stress caused by mismanaged emotions suppresses the immune system. Your body's ability to fight disease is directly correlated to the potency of your immune system, so this suppression increases your vulnerability to disease. Stress and anxiety are driven by the fear center in our brain. The fear center signals a threat in our environment that needs immediate attention. Energy is diverted away from the immune system to address the perceived threat. And all of this is due to emotions that have been mismanaged.

The following is a list of the benefits of having high emotional intelligence and effective social skills.

Higher self-esteem. Self-esteem is the emotional component of self-worth. Everyone needs to feel like they matter. Through the successful use of social skills, relationships become more gratifying, and we feel more validated with each successful social interaction. In turn, every experience of validation makes us feel like we matter and increases our self-esteem.

Feeling loved. Not only do we need to feel like we matter, we also need love. It is in relationships that we experience love. Love comes in many forms, and it takes different social skills to enhance each type. The better your social skills, the more types of love you can experience.

Oxytocin magic. Oxytocin is a hormone and neurotransmitter in the brain that is involved in relationship-building. It has been associated with lower stress and better physiological adaptation to high-stress situations. Trust, relaxation, and psychological stability are also correlated with oxytocin. The early stages of romance generate high levels of oxytocin. The pleasurable feelings we get from oxytocin—one of the brain's key "happy chemicals"—are all connected with social skills.

More career opportunities through a bigger network. People with high emotional intelligence have greater career success. One of the best ways to get a job is through networking, which requires social skills. New opportunities are more likely to surface as the size of one's network increases.

Feeling connected to the human community. Humans are dependent on one another for survival, and from this survival need comes our yearning to feel connected. Even if we are not geographically close to our loved ones, we feel more whole when we are in touch with them. When a loved one dies, it creates an emptiness in our life. Using social skills to maintain contact helps us appreciate our time together.

Peace due to a clear conscience. The human desire to please others is built into our DNA from childhood. In general, people cultivate a clear conscience when they treat others well. Not all interactions are easy, and not all conflicts are avoidable, but good social skills mitigate the challenges and bad feelings that may come with difficult interactions. This leaves us with a clear conscience and a feeling of peace.

Being understood. When we allow our emotions to get out of control, the "thinking" part of our brain becomes constricted, and the survival part of our brain takes the lead in guiding our behavior. When this happens, we are unable to think straight or behave in a prosocial way, and we struggle to communicate effectively. Effective emotional intelligence helps us manage our emotions so our brain functions remain balanced. This enables us to use good social skills and have positive social interactions even in the midst of escalated emotions. The end result is the ability to understand and be understood.

Better collaboration. The inhibition of the thinking part of our brain also limits the effectiveness of personal collaborations. We need our entire brain engaged in order to use effective social skills. When we can understand others' points of view and respond with appropriate levels of emotion, the result is a better collaboration.

OVERCOMING SOCIAL FEARS

Being introverted and inherently shy can certainly limit some social skills, such as assertiveness. In addition to introversion and shyness, there are recognized mental health disorders that can impact how people communicate. Sometimes, these mental health conditions, which may be clinically diagnosable, can interfere with interpersonal interactions, as well. In this section, we will discuss social skill limitations driven by personality types and mental health conditions.

INTROVERSION

Introversion is a personality type that presents as quiet, inward focused, thoughtful, and observant. Introverts tend to think to speak rather than speak to think. This means they will process issues for some time before communicating them out loud. When it comes to verbalization, less is more for introverts. When an introvert speaks, their words are well thought out and carefully chosen to get their message across in the most succinct and efficient way possible. In a group setting, introverts can feel like they have to compete to speak, which requires a lot of energy. As a result, their social skills may not be well honed, and the energy they require to use social skills may be limited.

The biggest challenge for introverts is understanding extroverts. It's a lot easier for extroverts to interact socially, and they assume introverts are just as motivated as they are to quickly respond to a situation with enthusiasm. Understanding an extrovert's world can help normalize an interaction and set expectations for an interpersonal encounter. On the flip side, an extrovert may also struggle to understand the mind of an introvert. Without this understanding and appreciation of what it's like to be an introvert, an extrovert may wonder if an introvert is depressed, angry, or simply withdrawn. By fostering awareness and understanding of both types of personalities, the odds of a successful relationship emerging are much greater.

SHYNESS

Shyness is the fear of speaking out and being seen. While introverts may simply prefer to be quiet, people who are shy experience a component of fear associated with speaking in public. Fear is one of the biggest obstacles to overcome to be effective with social skills. This is especially true if a person has had past experiences that were painful, awkward, or even traumatic. All of these factors can contribute to reinforcing shyness and ultimately short-circuiting social skill expression.

It is important to understand the organic and socially driven causes of shyness to properly address it. This understanding can be gained through reading about shyness or, better yet, going to therapy; in the therapeutic relationship, shyness can not only be understood but also treated. This happens because therapy is more than just a knowledge transfer. It is a real human relationship that is completely safe and allows people to experiment with and push against whatever blocks are limiting their social interactions. People can be wounded and healed in relationships. If something in a person's past is causing shyness to the point where they are missing out on social interactions, therapy might be just what they need. The good news is that with knowledge, practice, and proper treatment, a shy person can resolve their past experiences, and their social skills can flourish.

SOCIAL ANXIETY DISORDER

Anxiety disorders as a whole are the most common mental illnesses in the United States. These disorders impact more than 18 percent of the population each year. Anxiety disorders are treatable, yet less than half those suffering from these disorders seek treatment. When left untreated, an anxiety disorder increases the need for medical care and psychiatric hospitalization. Social anxiety disorder is a clinically diagnosable condition that may require professional treatment from a mental health provider. It is one of the most common of all the anxiety disorders.

Social anxiety disorder is characterized by an overwhelming fear of social situations and criticism. This fear or anxiety is out of proportion to any actual threat in a given social situation. To be diagnosed with this disorder, the anxiety must last six months or longer. Before embarking on a program to improve one's social skills, it is important that they evaluate the severity of their anxiety and, if necessary, seek medical treatment.

AUTISM SPECTRUM DISORDER

One way to understand autism spectrum disorder is to look at the word *autism*. Autism is derived from the Greek root, *auto*, which means self. Autism is an abnormal obsession with the self. This obsession manifests on a spectrum with varying levels of severity and multiple symptoms, which is why it is called autism spectrum disorder (ASD). Autistic behaviors range in severity across two major categories: (1) social communication and (2) restricted, repetitive behavior. The more severe the behaviors, the more support a person with ASD needs to function in social settings.

Limited levels of impairment include the following difficulties:

- **Challenges with initiating social interactions despite ability to speak in complete sentences**
- **Lack of responsiveness to social engagement initiated by others**
- **Difficulty with back-and-forth conversations**
- **Struggles with making friends**
- **Difficulty switching between activities and managing change**

More severe levels of impairment include the following difficulties:

- **Speaks in simple sentences**
- **A narrow range of special interests**
- **Very limited social initiation**
- **Responds only to direct social engagement**
- **Restricted repetitive behavior with high distress around change**

Because there is a spectrum of autistic behaviors, it is important that anyone who suspects they may have ASD gets a proper evaluation from a mental health provider. ASD shows up differently in every individual, and a mental health provider can explain how a person's specific condition can help or challenge them not only with social skills but with life in general. Getting a diagnosis is highly recommended because, from there, social skills training can happen at the right pace, with the right learning modality, and with the right expectations. ASD improves over time, and social fallout can be minimized with the proper support and diagnosis.

AVOIDANT PERSONALITY DISORDER

Nervousness and fear are core characteristics of avoidant personality disorder. People with this disorder experience strong feelings of inadequacy and have an intense fear of rejection and being judged by others. Their preoccupation with criticism and rejection leads them to avoid social contact, especially if there is a risk of not being liked. Their sense of inadequacy impacts all of their social interactions. A strong negative self-image (especially when it comes to social comparison) and an aversion to risk-taking or fear of failure characterize this disorder.

Friends are hard to come by, and loneliness is preferred over taking the risks needed to make social connections. If you have been diagnosed with this condition, it is important that you get professional treatment in addition to learning about social skills. Both psychotherapy and psychiatric treatment may be helpful with this condition.

PANIC DISORDER, GENERALIZED ANXIETY DISORDER, DEPRESSION, EATING DISORDERS, ALCOHOLISM, AND SCHIZOPHRENIA

Social skills require a common experience of reality to work. Mental health challenges can create significant obstacles for the expression and successful use of social skills. It is important to be properly assessed by a professional if you suspect that any of the following or other mental health conditions are blocking your ability to effectively use socials skills.

Anxiety disorders, such as panic disorder and generalized anxiety disorder, create challenges for social engagement. Panic disorder consists of recurrent, unexpected panic attacks along with a persistent fear of another panic attack occurring. Maladaptive behavior changes can also manifest in order to avoid perceived situations where a panic attack might occur. A panic attack is an acute state of fear that occurs abruptly. The attack is accompanied by physical and cognitive symptoms, such as racing heart, hyperventilating, fear of losing control, and sweating. Panic attacks can be expected or unexpected. In an expected panic attack, the cause is known, while an unexpected panic attack can arise out of nowhere for seemingly no reason at all.

Generalized anxiety disorder is characterized by a pervasive worry that persists for at least six months. This worry is difficult to control. Symptoms associated with generalized anxiety disorder include feeling on edge, irritability, tense muscles, and difficulty sleeping. Significant impairments in work, school, and personal functioning are also present, as well.

Depression is a mood disorder that can also interfere with socialization. Engaging others using social skills requires motivation, and motivation requires positive feelings to take action. Depression limits these positive feelings, which can eliminate or reduce one's motivation and, consequently, eliminate or reduce one's interpersonal social engagement.

Eating disorders and alcoholism are classified within the addictive behavior category. When an addictive behavior is dominant in a person's life, everything else becomes a lower priority. Engaging with other people in mutually beneficial behavior is replaced by the need to manipulate others to get what is desired.

Schizophrenia is a brain disorder that disconnects people from a shared reality with others. As a result, significant disruptions occur in a schizophrenic individual's interpersonal, academic, and professional life. To be diagnosed with schizophrenia, one must display at least two of the following symptoms over a one-month period: delusions, hallucinations, incoherent speech, disorganized behavior, and negative symptoms, such as reduced emotional expression (APA, 99). Schizophrenia creates a false reality for an individual that is separate from the reality of others.

GETTING COMFORTABLE

Five key factors that contribute to the success of social skills are confidence, forgiveness, self-compassion, self-awareness, and emotional awareness. A deficit in any of these areas will limit the effectiveness of your social interactions. In the following sections, we will define each of these factors and discuss ways to promote the enhancement of each quality.

CONFIDENCE

Confidence is the belief that one will achieve a positive outcome from an action targeted to reach a specific goal. For example, let's take a look at Frank, who is single and looking to get married. He is seeking to meet a woman with whom he shares chemistry and compatibility and hopes to form a relationship that will ultimately lead to marriage. Frank doesn't know any women he feels this way about at this point in his life, so he'll need to meet new women in order to find the right one.

The amount of confidence Frank has in his ability to present himself well and avoid awkwardness will have an impact on the effectiveness of his social skills. Frank's success will be impacted not only by his self-confidence but also the probability that he will engage with women at all. If Frank's confidence is low, then he will likely make excuses for not pursuing his goal of marriage. After all, it's not that he doesn't want to get married; he simply doesn't have the skills to do what it takes to pursue marriage.

How can Frank increase his confidence so he will take the risks necessary to meet a compatible partner? Frank needs to understand himself and be able to identify why he lacks confidence. Understanding oneself is no small task. Examining your own life is among the hardest tasks one can undertake. Many questions need to be asked, such as:

- **Have I always lacked confidence?**
- **Do other people in my family lack confidence?**
- **Is there anything that happened to me, such as rejection, that has decreased my level of confidence?**
- **In what situations do I feel the most confident? In what situations do I feel the least confident?**

A thorough self-inquiry by Frank—on his own or with a therapist—would help him understand his confidence issues. Once Frank gains a deeper understanding of his lack of self-confidence, a solid plan for increasing his confidence can be created. At that point, Frank will be in a better place to take risks and have greater confidence in using his social skills. He will also accept that social skills take time to improve, and he will be confident that, with enough practice, he will get better and be able to apply these skills to help him find a life partner.

FORGIVENESS/SELF-COMPASSION

Forgiveness and self-compassion are important antidotes to shame. Shame limits our ability to have peace of mind and good mental health. Our self-perpetuated negativity ruins our ability to start fresh and accept our past so we can create a new future. Shame tells us that it's not okay to be who we are. But humans constantly make mistakes. A life of growth is marked by learning from one's mistakes and trying again and again. Shame stops the growth process and tells us we need to give up and be miserable. It tells us that the process of learning and growing is futile. It is because of shame that forgiveness and self-compassion are so essential to well-being. We will struggle mightily to learn new social skills if we carry so much shame that we don't permit ourselves to make mistakes.

Frank, for instance, must forgive himself for the awkwardness he experienced asking girls out in high school. Adolescence is a difficult time of life as we navigate the path from childhood to adulthood. There's lots to be learned, and lots of mistakes are made along the way. Frank needs to let go of these past interpersonal moments by focusing on self-compassion. Forgiving himself and learning from his past mistakes is the most redemptive act he can do. What better way to learn about life than to learn from our own mistakes? Granted, this is no easy task. Our brains are primed to expect the worst and beat us up for not performing well. This helps us survive, but it doesn't make us all that happy.

It's been said that forgiveness and gratitude are the queens of the virtues; if you're not failing, then you're not trying hard enough. This is a fundamental principle of life. But nobody is perfect all the time. Learning how to forgive yourself is absolutely essential to being at peace and getting to a place of high motivation so you can try again.

SELF-AWARENESS

Most people operate on autopilot in their daily lives. It is only when something bad happens that they self-reflect. Autopilot is not an ideal state for self-awareness, as we blindly move through our day performing tasks we've done many times. Behaving this way makes sense because our brains are lazy. Our brains love habits because they have predictable results. The biggest problem with autopilot is that we don't learn and grow. We don't take time to understand why things happen and why we behave the way we do. We may react to situations defensively instead of with self-awareness. Defensiveness shifts the blame to the other person. It is only through self-awareness of our thoughts, emotions, beliefs, and behaviors that our lives become purposeful and meaningful. Only then can we step off the autopilot treadmill and become intentional thinkers.

Let's revisit Frank. If Frank is fantasizing about his partner and their 5 children 10 years down the road, he won't be grounded in the present and aware of what's happening in the moment. Without this knowledge of his immediate circumstances, Frank is in trouble. Social skills work best when both people are fully present in the moment. If Frank's thoughts are stuck in the past, ruminating over how he made a mess of his last date, he won't be fully present or aware of himself right now. If his thoughts are somewhere in the future, worrying if this person will want to see him again, he won't be fully present or aware of himself. Being grounded in the here and now is the best thing Frank can do to become aware of his thoughts, emotions, and sensations, which lead to self-awareness. Frank can then present the best version of himself, and this will allow him to socially engage more effectively.

EMOTIONAL AWARENESS

Many people struggle with awareness of their emotions. In my psychotherapy practice, I repeatedly tell my clients that they are not their thoughts and they are not their emotions; they are something much greater. In any moment, we can step back from our emotional experience and observe ourselves from a distance. It is this distance that gives us perspective and control over our emotions. A critical first step of emotional awareness is naming your emotions. Once you name them, you can have control over them. This is harder than most people think, but emotional awareness provides a big benefit to one's social skills. Emotional awareness is one part of emotional intelligence that leads to the advancement of social skills.

To do well with social skills, emotions must be part of the equation. Without emotions, our lived experience becomes rote and boring. During social encounters, emotions play a starring role because they are the driving force behind thoughts and behaviors. Just look around at people talking in a café. You will notice that their facial expressions and body language are powered by the back-and-forth exchange and the emotions that emerge from their shared energy. Don't shortchange emotions. They are at the heart of social skills and the experience that results from an interpersonal encounter.

So, how important will emotional awareness be for Frank? Dating is one of the most emotionally volatile and precarious endeavors anyone can embark upon. Frank will have lots of emotions, some quite intense, during this process. There is the excitement of attraction and romance and the anticipation of a life of intimacy and raising a family. The stakes are high, so the emotions are, as well. Frank will be much better prepared for this emotional adventure if his awareness of what he is experiencing is heightened. He will be able to identify the excitement when things are going well and the grief if rejection comes. In either case, with a high degree of emotional awareness, Frank will be able to separate himself from the emotion and, thus, be able to make sense of it. The best part of emotional awareness is the knowledge that all emotions are temporary. This is especially useful when going through difficult emotions. By developing his emotional awareness, Frank will be set up for success no matter what the outcome of his dating efforts is.

SETTING SOCIAL GOALS

Goal setting is where your journey toward improved social skills begins. The first step is to define what you want. Obtaining clarity on where you want to go is crucial for building better relationships supported by enhanced social skills. Prioritizing what you want simplifies life. But life is complex, and it's not easy to set clear goals. Why? Because goals force us to make decisions among competing desires. How much of a priority is it to improve your relationships by working on your social skills? Where does this goal fall within other goals in your life? When you have a clear goal, you are focused. What you focus your time, attention, and energy on is what gets done. In other words, the goals you create lead to the accomplishments you achieve. Your accomplishments are one of the key components of your overall well-being.

The goal of this book is to help you achieve your interpersonal goals. The tools within this book are practical guides that will help you achieve these goals. Once you've defined your goals, it's important to put in place a system that supports behavior that will help you reach them. This system can be thought of as an implementation goal. Human behavior is driven by repetition, so if there is a successful behavior we have repeated in the past, it is likely we will repeat it again. Again, our brains are lazy in that way. Why create a new behavior to achieve an outcome when we know a previous behavior worked just fine? That's why it is not enough to have an outcome goal; you also need to define an implementation goal or system that will help you reach your outcome goal. And the repetition that occurs through an implementation goal will foster the necessary habit change needed to reach your outcome goal of using effective social skills.

The following questions are designed to help you on your way toward social skills goal setting. I encourage you to write your answers freehand, using a pen or pencil. Writing by hand promotes a slow, thoughtful process that produces a meaningful result: a desire to own and believe in whatever goals you set for yourself. Carefully consider the following questions as a first step in your goal-setting task.

1. What are my social strengths and weaknesses?

2. Am I comfortable initiating and maintaining a conversation, or are conversations laden with anxiety? (This includes everything from eye contact to appropriate commentary to active listening.)

3. Do I enjoy interpersonal interactions?

4. Are there any upcoming events or relational encounters that could have a better outcome if I had better social skills?

   □ job interview
   □ presentation
   □ date
   □ negotiation
   □ sales call

5. When using my social skills, which of the following settings do I find easy or challenging? In which settings would I like to improve my social skills?

   □ socializing with friends I know well
   □ discussing a disagreement with my significant other
   □ public speaking
   □ having lunch with work colleagues
   □ running into an acquaintance on the bus
   □ making small talk with people I've never met at a work social

6. Are there any relationships in my life that are struggling? Am I working on improving them, or am I avoiding the problems?

7. Do I find it easier to initiate a social interaction or to respond to another person's social initiation?

8. Do I freeze when someone reaches out to me, afraid of not knowing what to do next?

9. Have I ever had, or do I have, a pattern of avoiding social situations?

10. Do I have any trauma or past wounds that might inhibit social interactions?

11. Do I need to forgive or ask for forgiveness because of a past wound that is limiting my ability to be in a relationship?

12. What are the pros and cons of remaining alone?

13. Do I want to let fear drive my social life?

CHAPTER 2

TYPES OF SOCIAL SKILLS

This chapter will explore four core social skills: verbal and written communication, listening, assertiveness, and empathy. It is important to take the time to explore these skills one at a time. By now, you may have realized that social skills are not as easy as saying what you want to say and then listening to what the other person says. If it were that easy, history would look quite different. Humans are complex, so it's no surprise that human interaction can be challenging.

VERBAL AND WRITTEN COMMUNICATION

Verbal and written language are the most obvious forms of communication. Have you ever tried to communicate with someone who spoke another language? Before instant translation software, this was a near-impossible task. Even sign language is a form of visual communication that is akin to verbal language. Spoken and written words have been the foundation of the human experience since early cave drawings. When technology emerged that allowed mass distribution of one's ideas, like the printing press or digital media, phrases surfaced that reflected the impact of this shift, such as, "The pen is mightier than the sword." The power of verbal and written communication needs to be respected and used wisely.

VERBAL

Verbal communication is the most common form of human communication. Humans speak an average of 16,000 words per day, according to a study in the journal *Science*. The most talkative person in the study uttered 47,000 words in a day, while the least talkative person spoke 700 words. The study explained that the differences between how men and women communicate revolve mostly around the content rather than the quantity of what each says. Women talk more about relationships, while men are more data- and gadget-driven with their content.

These gender differences are examples of unique interests and inclinations between people due to varying contexts. These differences are what make communication so difficult but also so fulfilling. When interpersonal gaps are bridged and coherent meaning is realized, it is then that the magic of oxytocin, which facilitates connection, begins. Cultivating the fundamental understanding and awareness that people are different and that we can't assume the other person understands us is the first step toward improving communication.

Written communication is fast and easy in our digital age, and it is replacing verbal communication more than it ideally should. Digital devices provide instant access to written communication, eliminating the cumbersome task of arranging face-to-face verbal communication. In his classic book *The Medium Is the Message*, Marshall McLuhan explains that not only is it important to consider the medium when communicating, but the choice of medium is actually more important than the message. A British Broadcasting Corporation (BBC) article inquired about the media we choose to communicate with. Are those choices saying anything about the message itself? The article explains the rapid explosion of text messages over email; we tend to associate email with office work and drudgery and text messaging with fun and intimacy. Emails are more structural, with "To" and "Subject" lines, while text messages are short, direct, and personal.

And then, there's paper-based communication. The tangible nature of paper combined with the security of it being offline has allowed it to remain a sought-after form of communication. An article reported that news found on digital media is more likely to be a hoax or misleading, while printed news offers a deeper exploration of a story. The sensory and tactile nature of paper remains unmatched compared to reading text on a digital screen. Consumers surveyed said they found reading print more enjoyable than reading from a screen. One of the most important lessons when using written communication is to choose your medium wisely.

LISTENING

Listening is the premier social skill. Are you an active or a passive listener? What is the difference between listening and understanding? When was the last time you felt like you were heard or even understood? Listening is a gift and an act of love when we give our time and energy to another person. Humans have two ears and one mouth for a reason. Listening and allowing room for silence provides the space needed for meaning to surface.

PARAPHRASE

Paraphrasing is an advanced skill of active listening. When you para-phrase, you are using your own words to repeat back what the other person has said. The value of this skill cannot be overstated. Keeping in mind that listening is a gift, what better gift can you give someone than restating what they said in your own words? Now, this might seem inefficient to some. Why would you repeat back what the other person just said? Because misinterpretation is common between humans. We have powerful egos that drive us to assert ourselves as competent and correct. This desire limits our capacity to slow down and really listen to what another person is saying.

Our ego craves praise and validation, and paraphrasing delivers that. The goal isn't to counter what the other person said but rather to validate them as a person. In the moment, think about what's more important: to be right or to affirm your partner's humanity and make them feel good? From this place of emotional connection, you are well positioned for a much more efficient and enjoyable discussion about the topic at hand.

CONSISTENT EYE CONTACT

Eye contact is a nonverbal form of communication that reinforces the verbal content being communicated during a conversation. Earlier, we discussed that communication is much more than a verbal exchange. Eye contact shows that a person is listening, and it is especially valu-able when making an important point or assessing whether a person is telling the truth. This is why, when they want a straight answer, people will ask you to look them in the eye and tell them the truth. It is hard to stare into someone's eyes and lie to their face (unless you're a socio-path). It's hard, in general, to stare into another person's eyes for a long time. Try it. Have a staring contest with another person, or try it with your dog first. That might be easier. Who won?

Eye contact, like touch, is a sensory experience that is connected to our emotional brain. All sensory experiences have an emotional compo-nent, which is why people love art, beauty, and sunsets. Eye contact is a powerful experience that goes beyond mere eyeball-to-eyeball interac-tion. It is a nonverbal way to connect with another person.

POSTURE

Posture falls into the category of body language social skills. Are you sitting up straight or hunched over? Is your posture open or closed? Are you facing your friend square or at an angle? All of these nonverbal cues send a message. Take a moment to consider if your posture is communicating the message you intend to send. A helpful mnemonic device to remember to facilitate proper posture and good nonverbal communication is the acronym SOLER. It is used to teach new counselors how to be effective when listening to patients.

S is for sitting at a distance and angle that is comfortable

O is for open posture with arms and legs uncrossed

L is for leaning forward at times and attentively listening

E is for effective eye contact without excessive staring

R is for remaining reasonably relaxed versus on edge

Posture is also related to appropriate body movements that can be used to respond to a remark. Listening is a dynamic activity.

OPEN QUESTIONS

Have you ever tried to talk to a teenager who isn't interested in talking to you? Do you get a lot of one-word answers? The trick to avoiding these types of responses is to be creative about how you ask questions. Open-ended questions are generally the best. There are many books and articles with examples of how to ask questions to teens, specifically, that will get them talking. It takes practice to be creative with questions. Another handy mnemonic device to remember that can assist you in social interactions when you are stuck is the acronym FEW.

F is for fact—ask another person to share a fact about themself, such as "What is your favorite hobby?"

E is for experience—ask about the person's experience when they are engaged in that hobby. What is it like? Why do they look forward to it?

W is for what—ask the person what the story is behind their hobby. How did they get into the hobby? What do they find interesting and enjoyable about it?

FEW is just one tool you can use to create open questions, an important social skill.

ALL ABOUT DETAILS

Closely related to asking open-ended questions is inquiring about details. Details are important when it comes to understanding people and how to present yourself to them. Your social skills will reach a new level of success when you pick up on details and integrate them into your responses. The devil truly is in the details, and if the details are not acknowledged and used in the ongoing conversation, the odds of success go way down. It is a challenge, but a rewarding one, to take the content of what a person is saying and paraphrase it back to them in a new way that maintains the integrity of what they are saying. This involves staying true to their original statement, which is encased in the details. It is hard to listen to all the details, but as an objective listener, you have a unique perspective to make sense of these details in a way that the speaker cannot. This dynamic is fundamental to creating shared meaning via effective communication.

MYTHS ABOUT ASSERTIVENESS

1. **Assertiveness is selfishness.** You are one unique instance of a human life that will never be repeated in all of history. Each person's fundamental task is to live out the unique life they have been given. How can you be yourself unless you have the courage to show up and own your thoughts, emotions, and values? This is not selfish but authentic. Authentic people are assertive; selfish people are more likely to be passive or aggressive. Aggressive communication leaves no room for the other person to present their thoughts. Passive communication does not engage in the effort it takes to create shared meaning. Assertive communication, by contrast, finds that balance between engaging in a conversation without overwhelming the other person.

2. **It's better to wait for others to take the initiative.** If everyone believed it was better to wait for someone else to take the initiative, then the world would be a very lonely place. Finding a balance of back-and-forth initiative is the ideal scenario for effective communication. Solid self-awareness enables us to know when it's time to assert ourselves. Awareness of others enables us to know when it's time to step back and allow them to take the initiative. Unfortunately, there are no simple answers about when the best time is to take the initiative. Communication is always give-and-take, like a dance where both partners are engaged in creating beautiful movements together.

3. **Nonviolent communication does not support being assertive.** Assertive communication, by its nature, is nonviolent. Nonviolent communication is best known for advocating "I" statements rather than "you" statements. For instance, instead of saying, "Why did you do that?", a nonviolent communicator would say, "I am wondering why you did that." It's a small but important shift in language. The "I" statement gets the point

across with the same clarity as the "you" statement, but it does so by emphasizing the speaker's experience of wonder and curiosity rather than putting blame on the listener. As a result, this focus shifts from accusation to education. The inquiry and challenge are still there, which keeps the speaker's position assertive, but the focus reduces the emotional intensity for the listener. This allows the listener to respond with more clarity and freedom.

4. **If I am assertive, then people won't like me.** Assertiveness is not the same as aggressiveness, and this myth is rooted in mistakenly regarding the two as the same. If you are aggressive, then it is very possible that people won't like you. For instance, bullies tend not to have many friends in the long run, even if they are compelling in the moment. When you are assertive, people will gravitate to you more because they know where you stand. They will value your thoughts even if they don't always agree with them.

5. **People who are introverts or have low self-esteem can't be assertive.** Assertiveness is a skill that can be learned and practiced. Start with something small. For example, if your neighbor has a dog that you know is friendly, practice approaching the dog in a friendly way that invites a response. The dog will most likely be happy with any attention and not be upset if you come across as awkward. Next, move on to engaging safe humans. Some humans are safer than others. The safest human interaction will likely be with a therapist, if you have one. Other safe people include those who are kind and compassionate by nature. Safe people are essential for introverts or people with low self-esteem when taking interpersonal risks. By taking incremental risks, your confidence will grow with each interaction. Your self-esteem will improve, and your world will open up as new relationship opportunities present themselves to you.

ASSERTIVENESS

You may be wondering, *How do I get my point across in a confident, direct, and clear way without coming across as aggressive, rude, obnoxious, arrogant, or offensive?* You can do it by being assertive. Assertiveness is the ability to communicate without being ambiguous, tentative, or uncertain about the point you are making. It is a better alternative to passive or aggressive communication styles.

A helpful metaphor to consider is a stage. Each type of communication style allows different people on stage. When you use a passive communication style, everyone is allowed on stage, but you're in the background, out of the spotlight. You play a supporting role and observe the performance. Have you ever had a conversation with someone you just met who dominates the conversation? You don't have much invested in the relationship, and you likely will never see this person again, so you go along until a reasonable exit presents itself. You use a lot of reflective listening and consistently put the focus back on the speaker. The dominant speaker may not notice what you are doing, as they may relish the spotlight and be unaware of your disengaged, passive style. This is an example of the other person being at the front of the stage and you playing the supporting role.

The opposite occurs when you use an aggressive communication style. In this situation, you are on stage, and no one else is allowed on. The conversation is now flipped; you are the dominant speaker who doesn't ask questions of other people. You constantly shift the focus back to yourself. There is little room for disagreement or challenge. You are the star of the show, and you are oblivious to everyone else's needs.

The assertive communication style occurs when everyone is welcome on the stage and has an equal role to play. You are entitled to bring your voice, as is everyone else. There is a give-and-take, as everyone brings their whole self to the performance. The choreography is magical, and the dance between the performers is seamless. Everyone has a unique role in this production, which gets rousing applause. Whether it's a play, team sporting event, or group project, the best outcomes occur when all the participants work well together, according to their abilities. Remember, there is no "I" in *team*—that's the assertive communication style.

Assertiveness is an expression of your authentic self. You can present your full identity in a way that does not minimize other people's ability to show up with their authentic selves. Your agenda is not threatening or judgmental but inviting and collaborative. Assertiveness moves a conversation forward toward a shared experience of dialogue where meaning is cocreated. Monologues are one-sided conversations and not collaborative, putting the focus on one speaker for an extended period of time. Monologues are the result of passive or aggressive communication styles. They are passive when one person allows the other person to do all the talking. They are aggressive when one person doesn't allow the other person to speak at all. Assertiveness is that happy middle ground where both people create something together, where they both strive toward the common goal of coherent shared meaning.

EMPATHY

To fully understand a message being delivered or an emotion being felt, we need empathy. Without empathy, we miss an important part of the equation that leads us to understand ourselves and others, which is fundamental to successful communication. Empathy plays a central role in helping us communicate effectively and make sense of our own emotions. Empathy is the visceral experience of another person's thoughts and feelings. Empathy for yourself is awareness of your own visceral experience of a feeling in the present moment. Within the tasks of understanding, communicating, and listening lies empathy, which connects us to our own and others' emotions and sets the stage for empathic communication.

Communication without empathy is a difficult venture. Fifty years of research on human communication has revealed that most communication is nonverbal. When we don't communicate our emotions, either verbally or nonverbally, words remain empty and are unable to create passion, which drives our and others' motivation to engage in the conversation. Empathy connects us with the emotions that infuse words with meaning, which, in turn, generates coherence. Coherent shared meaning is the goal of healthy communication. Certainly, words are important in this process, but it is the emotions behind the words that launch the communicators into a flow that allows for many views and precludes defensiveness. It is in this empathic, coherent state that intimacy and connection occur.

ACCEPTING EMOTIONS

The path to peace within ourselves and with others requires acceptance—acceptance of our own and others' emotions. Acceptance requires an understanding of why we and others feel what we feel and do what we do as a result of those emotions. An intentional journey toward knowing ourselves and others is an ongoing experience filled with gradually unfolding insights and revelations, all of which enhance and develop us as members of a larger social community.

We can accelerate the process of understanding through knowledge, introspection, and awareness of emotions. Reading this book is an excellent example of knowledge acquisition, yet it is not enough to understand ourselves and others. We need a healthy respect, perhaps even awe and wonder, for emotions.

Emotions are different from thoughts. Thoughts are easier to identify and name. It's the emotions behind the thoughts that make life interesting or challenging, depending on the emotion one is considering. Managing emotions is like nailing gelatin to a wall—no easy task! Yet it is these slippery emotions that we don't have total control over that give us the energy to live our lives.

PERSPECTIVE

Taking perspective is part of the process of empathy and is a skill that can be developed. Perspective allows us to walk in another person's shoes—that is, it enables us to view the world from the other person's vantage point. For example, if you are speaking with someone who is grieving the loss of a loved one, their emotions may be strong. There will likely be sadness in their voice and face. What if you understood their perspective? What if you could view the world from the place where that person is residing in that moment? This perspective would enable you to be present in a way that exudes understanding and lets the person know they're not alone. Perspective-taking involves knowledge and experience. Have I lost a loved one? What was my experience like? Do I know grief? All of these questions foster perspective. And all this begins with naming an emotion and being fully present with another person to understand their perspective.

NONVERBAL EMPATHY

Empathy, by its nature, is visceral rather than verbal (though that's not to say verbal skills cannot support and promote the work of empathy). As a psychotherapist, I encourage the use of nonverbal tools to facilitate empathy. For example, if two people are in conflict and one person's anger begins to escalate, that person is instructed to show a time-out sign or use a hand gesture. These are nonverbal ways to communicate that the person who showed the sign or gesture is in distress. These techniques express the covert emotion—in this case, anger—in an overt way to ensure that the other person receives the message that an emotion needs to be addressed. The showing of a sign or gesture can enhance the nonverbal experience of empathy.

There are times when a sign or gesture won't be understood or isn't appropriate. In these situations, we can use social reinforcer skills to convey nonverbal empathy. Social reinforcers include head nods, eye contact, facial expressions of approval, posture shifting, and even using sounds like "mm-hmm" or "oh." These nonverbal responses go a long way toward conveying empathy. They promote solidarity. They say, in a silent way, "You are not alone with your feelings." It is an act of love to journey with someone through an emotional experience, especially when the emotions are difficult. These practical nonverbal actions are foundational for any meaningful relationship.

We can choose to read a book, listen to a lecture, or think thoughts. Yet how do we tap into the little emotions that are the great captains of our lives? Emotions are not always logical. There is a certain mystery to them. What is needed is a way to engage with others—a pathway we can take toward understanding. This is the journey of empathy.

PART II

THE DEVELOPMENT OF CONVERSATION

In part 1, we laid a solid foundation for the necessity of social skills to drive effective communication and ultimately life-enriching relationships. Now, in part 2, we are going to dig deeper into the elements of a conversation. This will include specific skills for understanding body language, interpreting facial expressions, knowing your audience, making small talk, and navigating dreaded, difficult conversations. Acquiring knowledge about social skills is not enough. Applying that knowledge is critical to facilitate effective implementation of those skills.

CHAPTER 3

TUNE IN TO BODY LANGUAGE

While verbal and written communication sit at the core of a shared dialogue between humans, there is still more happening. In our age of artificial intelligence (AI), we hear stories of humans having conversations and even relationships with machines. These interactions are possible because an AI computer can generate sounds and words in response to a human. Conversations are foundational to any relationship—human or nonhuman. When we have a relationship with an animal, we have a conversation with it. It may not be verbal, but it is still an exchange of sensory information as we and the animal respond to each other. Nonverbal communication also plays a big role in human-to-human relationships. This chapter will explore what elements contribute to human conversation beyond the mere exchange of words.

ROLES OF NONVERBAL COMMUNICATION

Nonverbal communication includes facial expressions, body movements, interpersonal space, touch, and even how a person looks and what clothes they are wearing. All these factors are part of the communication exchange.

Behavioral scientists have struggled for decades to decode nonverbal communication and improve communication. Research has offered some surprising statistics, concluding that up to 93 percent of meaning is conveyed through nonverbal communication. This specifically applies when a speaker is talking about their feelings and attitudes. The importance of verbal versus nonverbal communication varies based on the content and intent of the conversation. Nonverbal observations become immensely valuable when you are trying to determine if you are being deceived or coerced. It is always useful to note when verbal communication is incongruent with the nonverbal messages. Nonverbal communication is central to the process of human information exchange; it regulates conversational flow, provides unsaid information about the speaker, and profoundly impacts the ultimate meaning of what is being conveyed.

A simple way to think of the roles that verbal and nonverbal communication play is that verbal communication is used for communicating information while nonverbal communication is used to support the relationship. The functions of nonverbal communication include the expression of emotions, personality, and attitude toward the other person. It also functions though rituals of greeting and departure, as well as supporting the interactive cues during the conversation. Some cultures have more nonverbal interaction than others, such as hugging, kissing, hand gestures, and eye contact. These cultures are considered high-context cultures.

Before delving further into nonverbal communication, let's review the classic communication model. It is defined as:

SENDER > MESSAGE > MEDIUM > RECEIVER > FEEDBACK

In this model, the sender delivers a message through a chosen medium to the receiver. Feedback is then given to the sender, and the process repeats. From here, we add the nonverbal elements of communication, which we will discuss in the following sections on facial expressions, body movement, interpersonal space, and touch.

FACIAL EXPRESSIONS

A person's face says a lot without even uttering a word. There is a static component of facial expressions, which is how the face looks. Cultural factors play a role here. Is the person attractive to you or plain? Think of the first moment of a date when you get an initial impression of the other person, which sets the stage for the encounter. The dynamic component of facial expressions involves the movements of the face and related body parts. What strikes you as attractive? What do you find annoying? Maybe a slight smile is endearing, while a facial tic is distracting or irritating.

THE EYES

For most people, their visual sense is dominant, and eye contact is an essential part of nonverbal visual communication. The eyes can be shaped and moved into many positions, and the eyebrows are also part of the presentation. A friend of mine used to have a signature expression where he lifted one eyebrow; everyone knew, at that moment, something important or challenging was being conveyed. There is a dynamic interplay between a person's eyes, such as when one eye is closed or both are open wide. A wink delivers a nonverbal message, for instance, that the verbal content is a joke or has special meaning. Wide-open eyes can convey surprise or shock. Rolling eyes indicate disbelief or disdain.

In addition to the position of the eyes, eye contact plays a major role in the flow of a conversation. Noticing a person's eye contact helps determine if the person is engaged and interested in the conversation. It is reassuring to find that the person's focus is on the discussion at hand and not lost in other thoughts. It's much harder to think of something else when looking into another person's eyes.

There is a flow and rhythm to eye contact. Staring too much or too intently is considered odd and rude, while not looking into the eyes at all can be taken as a sign of total disinterest. The eyes are connected to the optic nerve, which is in the back of the retina. The optic nerve is part of the nervous system. Nerves can only take so much stimulation before they need rest. Whether standing in ice-cold river water or staring into someone's eyes, nerves have a limit. Knowing your own limits and sensing the limits of others is part of the proper use of the eyes in nonverbal communication.

THE MOUTH

In addition to the eyes, the mouth is a major contributor to nonverbal communication. Expressions of the mouth cut across all cultures, from smiles to frowns to surprise to confusion. Paul Ekman found that facial expressions are among the most universal forms of body language. They communicate common emotions like fear, sadness, anger, and happiness. The mouth plays a pivotal role in expressing these emotions. No words are needed when these universal mouth movements appear. You might enjoy checking out a website that shows 15 common facial expressions; go to enkiverywell.com/facial-expressions-list.html. Look at each picture first and see if you can guess what message is being conveyed before reading the description. From biting one's lip to moving lips into extreme positions, mouth movements are universally accepted to mean certain emotions.

ARMS AND LEGS

Arms and legs are part of the nonverbal communication process as well. Crossing arms or legs might indicate defensiveness or an unwillingness to be vulnerable. Rapid movements of the arms or legs might indicate anxiety or feeling uncomfortable. Pointing can come across as aggressive. The position of the hands needs to be considered when communicating. For example, placing hands on the genital area sends a sexual or offensive signal. Hands on hips can mean a person is feeling in control and confident. It is important to note that these are general guidelines that don't always apply. One must consistently check for the congruence of the content, the environment, and one's gut instincts. And, of course, when unsure, you can always ask if what you are interpreting is accurate.

POSTURE

Posture refers to how an individual is holding their body in addition to the overall physical form of their body. We generally think of a posture as open or closed. Does the posture convey an openness to communicate, or is the individual shut down and closed to communication? Posture can tell us a lot about someone's current emotional state and well as personality characteristics.

Open Posture

An open posture can indicate friendliness and a willingness to engage, speak, and listen. An open position of the body signifies a welcoming stance toward communication. The trunk of the body tends to be exposed with an open posture. The individual will sit up straight and focus on you. Shoulders will be back, and the chest will possibly be out slightly. Think of someone sitting on a mat meditating. Meditators are taught to sit up straight with the chest out and the lumbar curved inward to its natural position. This posture creates an attentive but calm position that can do the work of focusing the mind and creating ample space to fill the lungs with breath.

Closed Posture

A closed posture can indicate dislike, distrust, disagreement, or hostility. It is displayed when a person covers up the trunk of their body by hunching, crossing their legs or arms, or turning away. This closed posture is precisely what is *not* recommended for meditators. Body movement and position directly impact our feelings and ability to focus. In addition, it is physically not possible to fill your lungs with air when you are hunched over, thereby restricting airflow to the far reaches of your lungs.

BODY MOVEMENT

Body movements and gestures, such as leaning forward, turning toward or away from another person, clenched fists, or folded arms, are all sending messages. These movements and gestures can add impact to your message or distract from it if they are incongruent with what you are saying.

LEANING FORWARD

The position of your body is an important piece of nonverbal communication. Leaning forward is one of the active listening techniques that uses body movements. When your body leans forward, it conveys interest and engagement. Leaning inward is similar to posture, as discussed in chapter 2 on page 25. A memory tool mentioned in relation to posture also applies to leaning inward. This acronym is SOLER:

S is for sitting at a distance and angle that is comfortable

O is for open posture with arms and legs uncrossed

L is for leaning forward at times and attentively listening

E is for effective eye contact without excessive staring

R is for remaining reasonably relaxed versus on edge

The L (leaning forward at times and attentively listening) is the primary reference here, though the other SOLER instructions also support active nonverbal engagement in the conversation. By leaning forward, the other person's concerns are being understood and validated by body movement and focus. Feelings of care and genuine interest emerge when one is affirmed and heard. It is on this foundation that one feels worthy and even loved.

HAND GESTURES

When we think of hand gestures, we might picture someone talking with their hands in a very animated way. Hand gestures include clenched fists, a thumbs-up, the peace sign, or the okay signal. It is important to be aware of the cultural meaning of hand gestures, as not all gestures are interpreted the same way in different parts of the world. For example, in the West, the okay signal means *okay*, while in certain parts of South America, it is a vulgar gesture.

FOLDED ARMS

Folded arms is a body movement that aligns with a closed posture. This can mean the person is unfriendly or disagrees with your points. It is important to note that folded arms alone may not be enough to interpret a person as closed off. Look for other nonverbal signals, such as facial expressions, to confirm a closed position. In some cases, a person might just find folding their arms to be quite comfortable.

TURNING TO FACE YOU

Shoulders should be positioned at an appropriate angle, which can change depending on the person. If one's shoulders are too square, it can come across as intimidating. If the shoulders are turned away too much, it can convey disinterest. In my experience, men seem to prefer more of an angle than women. Square shoulders should be interpreted according to each individual's needs and preferences.

INTERPRETING YOUR BODY LANGUAGE

What body language do you use during social interactions? How self-aware are you when you're communicating content and expressing emotions? Are these questions hard for you to answer? For many people, they *are* challenging inquiries. People tend to operate on autopilot without great self-awareness. This is true in daily living and communication. Consider the following questions to increase your self-awareness of your body language. Doing so will help you be more intentional with the messages you are sending.

1. **How much space is between you and different people you communicate with?**

2. **What type of hand gestures do you use when you're talking?**

3. **Do you actively make eye contact or look away most of the time?**

4. **Do you gesture with your mouth to communicate an emotion?**

5. **What are your arms and legs doing when you are communicating?**

6. **Would you say your posture is open or closed in social situations?**

7. **Are your facial expressions actively engaged in a conversation, or do they remain flat and fixed?**

8. **What topics and settings increase and decrease your expressions of nonverbal communication?**

When our emotions are high, we tend to react rather than act. Tense situations increase our emotional response and cause involuntary reactions, including facial expressions, body movements, or sudden shifts in eye contact. Reactions come from our emotional brain and inhibit our ability to act from a place of freedom. When we are free, we bring the best version of ourselves to a conversation. The best version of ourself usually wants a win-win outcome, whereas our emotional brain is primarily self-interested. Our emotional brain has a narrow focus of survival—that is, on what is best for us—making us less aware of the interpersonal dynamic, which includes the other person. All of the questions listed above increase our self-awareness and encourage us to seek what is best for ourself *and* the other person.

THE SPACE BETWEEN US

The space between people engaged in conversation is yet another important part of nonverbal communication. What message is sent by being close versus distant? Close proximity conveys a close relationship or more intensity. Distant proximity indicates that more safety is needed and that the conversation is riskier. How do you avoid awkward moments caused by too much or too little distance? Awareness of the other person's proximity preferences is needed. This can be a felt sense or a simple observation. What happens if you prefer a different amount of space than the other person? The safety created by distance overrides social needs. If you prefer more space, you can indicate this nonverbally by moving farther away. Sometimes, nonverbal messages are not received, so you may have to verbally ask the other person to step back. All of these topics are part of the field of *proxemics,* which concerns the distance between people as they interact. The following are three types of settings where the distance will change to send a message based on the definition of the relationship.

INTIMATE DISTANCE

The distance for an intimate interaction ranges from a few inches to a foot. In an intimate situation, there is a level of closeness that supports physical touch, soft voices, and a high degree of comfort with the other person. This level of closeness provides a tactile as well as verbal interchange that adds to the nonverbal communication.

SOCIAL DISTANCE

Social distance may be anywhere from a couple of feet to more than 10 feet. The amount of separation is largely driven by how comfortable the people in the interaction feel with each other. A coworker you see every day will communicate with you at a closer distance than the barista you see once a week when you get your latte.

PUBLIC DISTANCE

Public distance can range from 10 to 25 feet. Situations within this category include teachers in a classroom or an executive giving a presentation in a large boardroom. There is a lack of closeness in situations like these. After the class is over, for example, students may leave the room without speaking so much as a word to the teacher. There is an assumption that the teacher was speaking to all the students rather than a single individual. The teacher's public distance from the students supports that expectation.

MISREADING BODY LANGUAGE

Part of being human is making mistakes. Misreading body language can happen anytime to anyone, no matter how advanced your social skills are. The simplest recovery from failing to read a social cue accurately is to admit the mistake and apologize if necessary. For example, if you read from someone's body language that they want to greet you with a handshake but they actually want to give you a hug, upon recognizing your mistake, you can name it by saying, "Woops! Hugs are good—let's go there!" If you misread an emotional state, you can say, "Sorry, you looked like you were in a happy place today, but it actually may not be the best time to have this conversation."

1. **Misunderstanding the social cues used by another culture is a common mistake people make when reading body language.** For example, people in the United States tend to prefer to maintain a greater distance than people in Mexico. A Mexican who is unaware of this may have some awkward moments with Americans until they learn the social and cultural norms in the United States.

2. **Stereotypes may also create miscues when reading body language.** For instance, one may believe that all politicians are physically expressive. But belief in this stereotype may cause body language to be misread if you go to shake the mayor's hand and they is actually reserved and not physically expressive.

3. **Common gestures, such as greetings or hand gestures, are regular sources of disconnection and awkwardness.** There is a wonderful book on this topic titled *Kiss, Bow, or Shake Hands*. It is targeted at business travelers who are unfamiliar with the local customs in other countries. The book is over 600 pages long, which speaks to the complexity of cultural communication when it comes to body language.

4. **Context is another area that can cause body language to be misinterpreted.** If a person is preoccupied with a problem or not feeling well and you don't read that from their body language, you might greet them in an overzealous fashion that causes them discomfort, even if, in other circumstances, they might be open to being greeted in such a way. Connecting the context to the body language is important to avoiding social mistakes.

A NOT-SO-TOUCHY SUBJECT

Teenagers can be awkward when it comes to touch. This transitional stage of life is fraught with self-consciousness, self-esteem issues, and a lack of confidence. Physical touch is nonverbal communication, and it can be hard to decipher its appropriateness in a given situation. Adolescents already struggle with body image and identity issues. Add to that interpersonal touch expectations, and social encounters become even more complex. The most basic examples are greetings and good-byes. When does one hug, shake hands, or kiss? When is it appropriate to make your point by touching the other person on the arm?

Touch can be difficult to navigate. The first rule of thumb is to err on the side of caution when using touch with someone you don't know. That said, touch can be a very effective nonverbal tool for communicating. But using it can be risky. Be especially aware, if you reach out to touch a person, of how they respond to your action. Awareness of yourself and others is always the first step to improving social interaction.

Appropriate and inappropriate touch is governed by the relational context, the comfort of each individual with touch, and how close the two people are. Is this a personal or professional relationship? Has touch ever occurred before? Is the relationship intimate, platonic, or more casual (e.g., an acquaintance rather than a friend)? Some people with sensory sensitivity issues are averse to touch and uncomfortable with it. No matter how well you know the person, and no matter what the context is, touch is not welcome. The current level of connection and closeness also guides the appropriate use of touch. Two people may be married but living with an unresolved longstanding conflict; in this circumstance, one or both spouses may not want to be touched by the other. Beyond awareness of yourself and others, the three areas to consider when using touch as a form of communication are context, comfort, and closeness.

CHAPTER 4

GETTING CONVERSATIONAL

D ifferent settings dictate different conversational goals. Work environments are task-oriented and structured, while personal settings are more informal and familiar. The goal of a work setting is productivity, while the goal of a personal setting is relational. Different settings call for different social skills, and becoming familiar with a variety of social skills will prepare you to use the right skills in a given setting. This chapter will explore the components of social skills within conversations that can be applied to different settings.

THE RULES OF ENGAGEMENT

Following basic etiquette in conversation is job one. The rules of engagement for a conversation set the tone for the whole experience. It is important to remember that conversations are much more than the words being spoken. As discussed previously, nonverbal and para-verbal communication are even more important. Hence, the rules of engagement can set an energetic tone and keep the emotions positive during the conversation, both of which make it easier to communicate one's message effectively.

KNOW YOUR AUDIENCE

Not all audiences are the same; in fact, they can differ widely from one another. There is an old saying about public speaking: An amateur public speaker knows their speech, while a professional public speaker knows their audience. You may have prepared the best speech in the world, with brilliant examples and flawless logic that delivers a convincing argument, but if your audience does not have the educational background to track your reasoning, the speech will fall flat no matter how great it is.

It is critical to know your audience. Are they an acquaintance, a friend, a stranger, a colleague? What interests that person? Do they prefer formal or informal language? What types of nonverbal communication work well with that person? Salespeople are trained extensively to know their audience. Different personality types respond to different sales approaches. A myriad of personality assessments have been developed to understand our personalities. This knowledge is essential to explain behavior and to learn what makes us happy. Know thyself and know thy audience. This is where the rules of engagement begin.

THINK BEFORE YOU SPEAK

One of the most popular personality tests is the Myers-Briggs Type Indicator (MBTI). The MBTI is made up of four scales. One of the scales is introvert versus extrovert. Introverts are internal processors. They get renewed through time alone and do a lot of thinking before speaking. Thinking before speaking is a useful trait for anyone, introvert or extrovert. Extroverts tend to speak to think, so they have a harder time thinking before speaking.

Are you an introvert or an extrovert? Do you naturally think before speaking, or are you more inclined to speak before thinking? There are many free MBTI tests you can find online (e.g., Truity.com). Knowing your MBTI personality type will be a helpful guide as you embark on your journey to improve your social interaction skills.

NAVIGATING DIFFICULT CONVERSATIONS

Difficult conversations (e.g. crucial conversations or courageous conversations) are not easy. They can be nerve-racking and create a palpable sense of fear and anxiety. Navigating these conversations is best done with a plan for success. Otherwise, the fear and anxiety we experience during these conversations can be overwhelming and make us want to avoid them in the future. The following protocol is an example of a plan that can increase your odds of successfully handling a difficult conversation.

1. **Set up the conversation.** This step is a precursor to the difficult content that needs to be discussed. It creates an emotional bridge to your conversation partner that is essential before delivery of the content. A setup statement looks something like this: "Hi, Fred. I have an issue that is causing me some stress. I'm wondering if you could help me with it?" Without a setup statement, the conversation begins like this: "Hi, Fred. When you keep leaving the toilet seat up in the bathroom, I get stressed out. Why do you keep doing that?" Start with a setup statement and prepare the ground for engagement. It will be easier for all parties.

2. **Learn about the issue.** Your biggest ally in this step is curiosity. Be curious and learn about the issue. Use learning statements to build upon your knowledge. For example: "Help me understand why my leaving the toilet seat up stressed you out. I'm really curious." The opposite of a learning statement is a blaming statement, such as this: "I don't understand why you get stressed out by the toilet seat being up. It's not that big of a deal." Learning is always better than blaming.

3. **Set down the conversation.** Now that you've learned about the issue and built an emotional connection, it is time to close the conversation. This involves summarizing what you have learned and planning what needs to be done next. An example of a set-down statement is "I've learned a lot about why leaving the toilet seat up stresses you out. When you are tired and need to use the toilet, it's hard to remember to check the toilet seat. I think we should figure out a way for me to remember to put it down. Can we talk about that next time?" It is common to simply skip this step, but it is important to promote a graceful rather than hostile exit from the conversation. The former will support the relationship, while the latter will wound it.

WAIT YOUR TURN

Conversations should be dialogues, not monologues. Successful dialogues have equal input from both people involved. There is a back-and-forth to a dialogue that creates an energetic experience that benefits both participants. Dialogues create something greater than what any one individual could create on their own. Part of this mutual investment in creating shared meaning is a give-and-take process. This process requires each person to wait their turn to speak. This back-and-forth involves listening, then speaking, then listening again.

Active listening takes effort. When you've listened well, you have received a message that is hopefully close to what the speaker intended. Waiting your turn is not about waiting until your partner's lips stop moving; it is about waiting until a message has been received and understood. Ideally, the speaker will pause when they have delivered a complete message. It is in this space that the other partner now has an opportunity to speak. A back-and-forth dialogue depends on both people waiting for the proper moment to speak, and then taking their turn.

ASK QUESTIONS (BUT NOT TOO MANY)

Asking questions is a wonderful way to spark conversation. Questions are at the heart of human inquiry and learning. They reveal where our focus is and have immense power to shape our lives and the conversations we have with others. The quality of the questions we ask showcases the quality of our inner world and, ultimately, the quality of our life. If you want better answers, then ask better questions. Instead of asking negative, self-defeating questions that kill conversations, ask positive, life-affirming ones. For example, instead of asking, "Why did this horrible event happen to us?" ask, "How can we bounce back from this difficult situation?".

It is also important to avoid asking too many questions. You don't want the conversation to turn into an interrogation. Keep in mind the back-and-forth process described in the previous section. Remember to pause and listen; give your partner a chance to offer input. Rapid-fire questioning doesn't allow the time and space needed to go deep into a subject in a mutually satisfying way.

HONESTY

The absence of honesty in a conversation creates obvious problems. If the goal of communication is to create something in common, then the thing created cannot be built on lies and falsehoods because trust will ultimately be eroded. Consequently you will lose interest since the probability that your conversation partner is being truthful is low.

Honesty in thoughts as well as emotions promotes successful dialogue. In my psychotherapy practice, I regularly encourage people to notice their emotional state as they are having difficult conversations. Awareness of and honesty about one's emotions builds credibility and trust. Granted, it requires a certain amount of vulnerability to be honest. Yet vulnerability is the gateway to intimacy. If you desire connection and intimacy, then vulnerability and honesty are foundational to this relational experience. If you desire competitive relationships, then it may be more tempting to be dishonest. However, in both intimate and competitive relationships, honesty always serves the common good most effectively.

AVOID OVERSHARING

While under-sharing in a conversation handicaps the outcome, there is also a danger to oversharing. There is no scientific formula to determine how much is too little to share and how much is too much. This requires a felt sense of appropriateness that comes with practice. Part of achieving this sense of appropriateness is having a sense of how well the conversation is going for each person. Self-awareness tends to be easier than other-awareness, so a good place to start is asking yourself how the conversation is going for you. Do you feel like there is an imbalance in the amount of content you are sharing versus the amount your partner is sharing? Or do you feel there is a happy balance in place? Assessing the conversational flow begins with knowing your natural inclination. Are you a stronger talker or a stronger listener? If you tend to talk a lot, be wary of this and check in regularly with yourself as the conversation progresses.

LEAVE YOUR EGO AT THE DOOR/AVOID "ONE-UPPING"

Conversational flow can be disrupted if one's ego gets in the way. The ego is the part of ourself that wants to appear important, valuable, and competent. When the ego needs excess validation, it can show up in aggressive, antisocial ways. This is not helpful for creating common shared meaning in conversations. Do you want to be right, or do you want to experience a fruitful dialogue where everyone wins? If being right is always more important to you than a healthy dialogue, your relationships will suffer. This doesn't mean you can't have opinions, of course, or share what you believe to be true. Once again, it is about creating a healthy balance with your conversation partner. Am I genuinely listening to their point of view? Am I giving my partner equal time to share their ideas compared to mine? If an imbalance exists, be wary of a possible ego agenda that wants to be right and affirmed at the expense of a rewarding dialogue.

PHRASES TO AVOID

The following five phrases should be avoided during a conversation, as they may either offend or disengage your partner. Alternative phrases that won't offend are provided for each, as well.

1. **Am I boring you?** This is a very direct question that could be offensive and create an awkward feeling in the person being asked, as it suggests they are not being attentive. Here is good alternative to this question: "I'm sensing that you are tired or distracted. Should we continue our conversation later?" This approach broaches the idea that the other person may not be fully engaged while avoiding a direct question and the use of the emotionally laden word *boring*.

2. **You already said that.** This is another potentially off-putting statement. While it may be true that the person is repeating themself, there are better ways to communicate this observation. For example, "I think you said this already. I'm guessing this is an important point for you." This gets the message about repeating across but softens the delivery by offering a possible explanation for the repetition using an "I" statement (see the discussion of "I" statements on page 27).

3. **Have you had any plastic surgery?** This is an extremely personal question. Unless you are very close to this person and deep trust has been established, this is a risky question. If the individual offers that they had plastic surgery, you might inquire about it in a more general way; for instance, you could say, "That's interesting that you decided to get plastic surgery. Was it a good experience for you?" Notice the broad nature of the question—it's neither too specific nor too personal.

4. **You're not making any sense.** This is an accusatory statement that can provoke a reaction. Your conversational mission is not to attack but to collaborate. It may be true that the person you

are talking to is not making sense, but there are better ways to say that. An alternative to this statement is: "I'm struggling to follow you—can I ask some questions just to clarify?" This statement invites collaboration and also offers a solution to the problem. The statement is honest and benevolent, whereas the original statement is honest but not benevolent.

5. **You're not listening to me.** This statement can come across as an accusation, which can trigger defenses in the other person. Once defenses are triggered, the conversation tends to fall apart. Here's an alternative to this statement: "I'm feeling like you are not hearing me correctly. Could you help me understand if I'm getting my message across in a way you can hear?" This approach invites the other person, in a gentle way, to respond to your experience of not being heard, and it does so without triggering ego defenses that may react with an attack.

SMALL TALK

Small talk is part of just about every conversation. It sets the tone for connection and establishes a comfort level for moving on to more substantive topics. Whether you are at the grocery store, at work, or in a personal setting, small talk plays the role of connecting people. Executives at a business meeting, for instance, will engage in small talk at first, but the meeting will quickly move to focus on more agenda-driven topics.

Small talk is important for building social skills. Small talk is meant to be fun, and people like to have fun. Humor can be an effective way to promote fun, and small talk provides a great opportunity to say something funny. People also like to be asked about themselves, so another great way to engage in small talk is to ask about the other person.

Small talk is meant to connect people emotionally. Why do people say, "How are you?" when they don't really want a long, drawn-out answer to this question? Because it's part of small talk. Have you ever tried to open a conversation by jumping right into a topic? In some cases, this may be necessary, but it is very abrupt since it skips the emotional connection that is needed to share other content in the conversation. Small talk is the doorway to successful conversations because it attends to the human emotional experience that is the foundation of fruitful dialogue.

SMALL TALK CHEAT SHEET

Incorporating small talk into daily conversation does not have to be difficult. With a few tips and some practice, small talk can be a regular part of your social skills toolbox. The following are common small talk strategies and situations where they can be used.

1. **Simple greeting.** A simple greeting can be very effective when done assertively. Say, "Hello, I'm [your name]." Hold out your hand in a firm position, look into the other person's eyes, and smile. Practice holding your hand out with strength. Don't let your fingers wobble all over the place; keep them firmly together. A simple greeting can be used in any situation where you are meeting people.

2. **Commonly shared topics (weather, sports, news).** Common topics provide another way to make small talk. You could say, "I can't believe the windchill today!" or, "Can you believe the Red Sox are in the World Series again? I never thought they'd make it this year." Either remark provides an opportunity for the other person to join in a conversation that covers common knowledge. A situation where there is ample time to connect socially is a good place to use this approach. This could be a social gathering after work or a wedding reception. In these examples, you may know your coworkers well, but if the wedding reception is large, there may be many people you do not know. The beauty of common topics is that they work in both situations. These topics are part of our shared human experience and are useful in many different social settings.

3. **Connection to or role in the current setting.** Another way to engage in small talk is to ask, "What brings you to this event?" This establishes a connection within a network of people. Naming anything shared in common is always a good approach to small talk. This strategy can be helpful when there is a common reason for people to be in the same place.

4. **Closed-ended question.** A closed-ended question seeks a simple yes-or-no answer; for example, "Did you get to exercise earlier today?" Such questions can be helpful if you have confidence that the other person will invest in the conversation without your working too hard to get it going.

5. **Open-ended question.** Open-ended questions are good when you are trying to draw out the other person more by getting them to elaborate on a topic. This is a helpful strategy when there is uncertainty about how much the other person will say in response to your question. Adults talking to teenagers find this strategy helpful, as teenagers generally become less interested in talking to adults over time.

6. **Association.** Associative thinking involves one person coming up with a thought that relates to what the other person just said. For example, if a coworker said, "I just got back from a trip to Alaska," you could say, "That's fantastic! I traveled up the Inside Passage a few years ago. How did you enjoy your trip?"

CONVERSATIONAL FLOW

All conversations share a similar structure. This means we can deconstruct a conversation and identify its different parts. Once we do this, we can put the pieces back together in a way that provides an effective structure for any number of situations. Whether you're talking with friends, coworkers, or new acquaintances, the conversational flow will proceed along a predictable path.

Conversational flow begins with nonverbal interaction. When eyes meet or a smile is visible or a hand is extended or a high five is offered, it is seen as an invitation to communicate. At this point, energy is focused on an interaction with the other person. The conversational flow has begun.

This initial interaction is part of building the connection. Once that connection is established, the conversation continues in a way that holds interest for both people. This is where the back-and-forth dialogue occurs, with each person contributing to the shared meaning they are creating. If shared meaning is successfully created, then interest will be maintained. Eventually, interest in the conversation will wane, and it will move toward an ending. This is an energetic experience that both people usually feel. However, sometimes only one person may feel like the conversation is winding down. That's okay, but it does require clear communication, verbally or nonverbally, that an end is desired.

These three phases of a conversation—building the connection, holding interest, and ending the conversation—will be discussed in greater detail in the following sections.

THE NAME GAME

Remembering a person's name is a valuable social skill that builds connection. Not only remembering someone's name but also saying it can deliver validation and show interest: *Someone cares enough to know my name; I have value.* Using someone's name is a simple but powerful social technique. People perk up and listen more when they hear their name. It's a natural response. Leverage this response to support the journey toward building your social skills.

Here are some techniques for remembering people's names:

1. **Use the person's name soon after you hear it.** For example, after being introduced to Barney, you could say, "Nice to meet you, Barney. I'm interested in learning more about your work."

2. **Repeat the person's name in your head after hearing it.** Say to yourself, "Barney, Barney, Barney," while looking at him.

3. **Associate something about that person to their name.** For example, if Barney has a red tie on, you could say to yourself, "Barney, the red tie man." This is a catchy phrase that will help you remember Barney and his red tie.

BUILDING THE CONNECTION

Connection is where the conversational flow begins. This is where your small talk skills will be used extensively. Whether you are using a simple greeting, shared topic of interest, open- or closed-ended question, or a shared association, the connection needs to be established before you can move on.

Nonverbal communication is especially important because first impressions are a big deal. The other person will feel your energy if your nonverbal communication is strong and assertive. If you say, "Hi, my name is [your name]" with a limp handshake and falling tone, it is unlikely the other person will be all that excited to talk to you. But if you say, "Hi, my name is [your name]" with a firm handshake, eye contact, and a strong tone of voice, the other person is much more likely to perk up and take notice. At this point, the connection is heading in the right direction. From here, you can use further small talk techniques (see the Small Talk Cheat Sheet on page 59) to get the other person talking and build a foundation for topics of shared interest that could be useful to explore.

HOLDING INTEREST

Holding interest is the stage at which the conversation either moves forward or ends quickly. Active listening and inviting questions are central to the holding interest phase of the conversational flow. When you are struggling to think of what to say next, employing active listening is always a good strategy. Active listening includes three main components: social reinforcers, repeating, and paraphrasing. Social reinforcers include head nods, *mm-hmm* statements, and other verbal and nonverbal cues that indicate you are listening intently. Repeating is simply picking out words the other person has said and repeating them. If a person says, "I found the food at dinner to be stale and tasteless," you can reply, "Stale and tasteless!" This will cue the person to expand on those adjectives. Paraphrasing is taking what the person said and putting it into different words. For example, you could reply to the dinner comment, "Sounds like the food was a real letdown for you."

Questions are also essential to holding interest. These will flow naturally from active listening. Returning to the example where someone told you their food at dinner was stale and tasteless, you might want to know what was served: "What was served that was so stale and tasteless?" The person might reply, "Salad with wilted lettuce and lasagna that was stiff as cardboard." Now you've got some descriptive language to work with. You might want to know next how the person reacted after eating the food: "How did you feel afterward? Did you get sick?" At this point, the conversation is headed in a more engaging direction that is likely to hold the interest of both sides.

HOW TO IMPROVE THE CONVERSATION

The following are 10 easy tips that can be used to improve the flow of a conversation in any situation.

1. **Use good nonverbals, including eye contact.**

2. **Take a deep breath before you speak so your words are clear and strong.**

3. **Use good social reinforcers (head nods, *mm-hmm* statements, appropriate facial expressions).**

4. **Repeat key words the other person uses for emphasis and expansion.**

5. **Paraphrase when possible, using your own words to reflect back what the other person said.**

6. Ask good questions by focusing on a point the other person has made that interests you and asking about it.

7. Use associative thinking to connect thoughts.

8. Use hand gestures to emphasize points.

9. Use self-disclosure when appropriate; getting personal increases interest, as it is more relevant.

10. Cultivate awareness about your own and the other person's energy level; know when to move toward the end of the conversation as energy levels start to dwindle.

THE ENDING

As soon as you begin a conversation, every moment brings you closer and closer to its end. Do not take a graceful ending of a conversation for granted. Conversations that end gracefully leave a positive lasting memory in everyone's emotional memory. One of the biggest challenges in ending a conversation gracefully is knowing where to end it. Is my partner going to have the last word or am I? How do I indicate that I'd like to leave this conversation? These are key questions to ending a conversation. Without practice, ending a conversation can be awkward.

Like beginning a conversation, much of the success with the ending of a conversation is managing energy or emotions. This can be done verbally, nonverbally, or with paraverbal signals. For example, if you say, "It was so great to connect with you, Barney," and your tone of voice falls at the end, it's quite clear by the content and the paraverbal tone that you would like the conversation to end. However, if your tone goes up on the word *Barney*, it may seem like you have a question for Barney.

Nonverbal actions like a handshake, wave, or physically moving away are all signals that the conversation is ending. These actions, combined with some sort of verbal statement that brings closure, are great ways to end a conversation. The important point is not to indicate that another question or statement is coming. If all this fails, you may have to state clearly that time is up: "Barney, I have to go now, but it was great talking to you." This statement provides clear information that you have to leave, which implies the conversation is now ending. Adding an affirmation at the end delivers a parting emotional boost to the encounter. This is always a positive gesture that supports prosocial interaction. Of course, you also want to be honest. If it was not great talking to Barney, you might simply wish him a pleasant evening. There is no one way to end a conversation, but closure is an important phase of all good conversations.

PART III

PUTTING PRACTICE INTO PLAY

In the next part of this book, we are going to explore the use of social skills in specific types of relationships. These include friendships, dating, workplace interactions, and group interactions. While all of these types of relationships require many common social skills, there are different experiences and expectations within each of them, as well. So, we are going to look at these relationships individually, examine the components that make each one unique, and discuss the social skills you can use—and how to use them—in various scenarios.

CHAPTER 5

FRIENDSHIPS

I n our competitive, individualistic world, friendships often take a back seat to other priorities. In such a climate, it remains important to take the time and effort to develop and nurture truly deep and lasting friendships. In this chapter, we'll discuss how to find and grow your connection to friends by applying social skills. Three types of friendships will be referenced: a close friend, an activity friend, and an acquaintance. A close friend is one you can be vulnerable with, are in contact regularly with, and can call upon in a crisis. An activity friend is one with whom you have experiences that you both enjoy. This is a situational friend you can have fun with, but you wouldn't necessarily have deep conversations with them outside of the shared activity. An acquaintance is someone with whom you share a greeting, joke, or quip when you see them but nothing beyond that. We tend to have fewer close friends than activity friends and acquaintances. But be grateful for all your friends, as each one adds different values to your life.

FINDING FRIENDS

Finding friends in a digital age should be easy, but clearly the data says otherwise. Our society is more connected than it's ever been, but people are lonelier than ever before. Recent statistics report that almost half of American adults are lonely. Are you one of them? You don't have to be. Technology provides many ways to meet people. From meetup groups to social media to dating sites, the opportunities to connect with people abound. And there are plenty of opportunities to meet people the old-fashioned way—face-to-face. Whether it's athletic organizations, hobby clubs, special interest gatherings, or church groups, there is no shortage of ways to connect with others. The biggest challenge we face is moving from a random connection to friendship. This is where social skills come in.

Assertiveness is your greatest ally when finding friends. The biggest obstacle to assertiveness is low self-esteem. Assertiveness requires a bit of confidence that will enable you to take a risk. Finding friends requires joining in and reaching out. This is true both in person and on digital platforms. The following action steps are ideas you can use to be assertive and initiate interaction with a potential friend:

1. Observe your surroundings and find something that grabs your attention. This could become the current topic in a discussion thread or group conversation. Ask someone new a question about that topic.

2. Consider what you find interesting or attractive about one person in particular. Formulate a question about what you notice. For example, "Hey, Frank. Did you say you went to Harvard for undergrad?"

3. Use associative thinking to start a conversation. Listen closely to another person's comments or, if it's written conversation, read what they are writing about. Then, take a moment to observe a related thought that comes into your head. For example, if another person is speaking or writing about their vacation to the Bahamas, your recent trip to Belize may be relevant, and you can say, "Hey, Frank. Your vacation sounds amazing. I did some snorkeling off the coast of Belize once, and that reminds me of your trip."

DEEPENING FRIENDSHIPS

Friendships grow and deepen through vulnerability. Digital communication allows us to protect ourselves from awkward social mistakes or revealing parts of ourselves that we are not proud of. Friendships can only develop so deep on social media, which is why we need to move beyond text messaging. We need to be authentic to ourselves and others. It is only through our ability to show up authentically that friendships can flourish. But being vulnerable and authentic can be challenging. For someone who is uncertain about their social skills, it can be scary.

The most practical way to deepen friendship is to learn more about the other party by listening and asking questions. Think about the last time you felt someone really cared about what you were saying. How did it feel? When others listen to you and you to them, a mutual feeling of safety develops. Out of this place of safety comes the ability to take risks, to be vulnerable, and to be authentic.

Being vulnerable and authentic can be quite difficult. If you struggle with obstacles that limit your ability to deepen friendships, seek out a therapist or wise mentor to help you treat the pain that keeps you from being real. The joy of a deep friendship only comes after risk-taking and vulnerability. Combine that with deep listening and empathy, and you will be well on your way to genuine friendship.

SUPPORTING YOUR FRIENDS

Your willingness to support friends in difficult times is a gift to them. Providing support can manifest in different ways, depending on how close you are to that friend and your individual values. Are you someone who can be called upon when others are in a time of need? Are you generous with your time and resources? True friendships deepen in times of need. Of course, there are no guarantees that your friends won't ask for your help when it is inconvenient for you. But friendship involves sacrifice.

Empathy is a critical social skill when it comes to supporting friends. You will need to understand what your friend is going through to be truly moved to help. The word *compassion* means "to suffer with." Are you willing to be in solidarity and suffer with your friends when support is needed? This sacrifice is very meaningful for you as well as supportive of the relationship. Without empathy, it will be hard to pick up on times when your friend needs support. They may even think you just don't care. Err on the side of asking too many questions about how your friend is doing versus not asking enough questions, especially if you are not naturally gifted with affective empathy.

A handy phrase to remember when practicing empathy is "It sounds like . . ." There are a few variations of this phrase, such as "It seems like . . ." or "It feels like . . ." but all of them set the stage for active listening reflection. These phrases serve as launching pads for delivering an empathic response. For example, "It sounds like you are really frustrated" or "It feels like you are still grieving the loss of your pet." Each phrase starts with a statement that puts the focus on you, and then moves to your understanding of the other person.

Not all statements of empathy will be correct. You might say, "It seems like you are excited about your new job," when the person is actually just happy that they are no longer at their previous job. Don't worry about accuracy in your empathic responses. People will appreciate that you are trying, and it is okay to get it wrong from time to time. It is much better to try and fail when it comes to empathy than not to try at all.

ASKING A FRIEND FOR HELP

The flip side of supporting your friends is asking a friend for help. Our individualistic, competitive society promotes self-sufficiency, and many of us find it easier to call a taxi for a ride to the airport than ask a friend. But sometimes, we need help that only a friend can provide. Even so, asking for help can be hard because it requires us to admit we can't do something alone, and that makes us feel vulnerable. And when we feel vulnerable, we can find it difficult to express ourselves. How can we use our social skills to ask a friend for the help we need?

Asking for help requires being assertive, a social skill discussed in chapter 2 (see page 21). Assertiveness gets our point across in a benevolent way. The truth is spoken in a way that is inviting, warm, and direct. When we are honest with ourselves and others, good things happen. Assertiveness can also support or weaken the relationship, depending on its strength. If an assertive request for help is received well and an honest response is given, the relationship is strong. If assertiveness is received with defensiveness or avoidance, the relationship may be weaker than you thought. And now you have new knowledge about the state of that relationship. This knowledge can assist you in a decision to invest more or less in that relationship in the future.

What happens if your assertive request is rejected? What happens, for example, if Frank does not have time to help you move but does not offer a clear, assertive response? This leaves the relationship in limbo. Rejecting a request from a friend is hard because people naturally want to please each other. Frank could reject your request clearly and assertively by being honest by using one of the following statements:

- **"I'd love to help you move, but my boss wants me in the office all weekend."**
- **"I am so beat from the week, but I can help if you don't find anyone else."**

Each of these examples is honest. The first example provides a legitimate schedule conflict, and the second is sincere about Frank's energy levels but also says he will assist you if need be.

Defensive or avoidant responses imply that Frank is unable to be honest or he does not value the relationship. Examples of defensiveness or avoidance are:

- **"People always ask me to help them move."**
- **"I'm not sure yet. Let me see how my schedule plays out."**

In the first example, Frank is defending himself against even being asked in the first place. In the second example, Frank simply delays the response, hoping the situation at hand will go away. Relationships thrive when people are honest and transparent while also being assertive.

LONGEVITY IN FRIENDSHIPS

The strength of friendships can increase or decrease over a period of time. While a positive interaction may strengthen a relationship, a negative interaction can weaken it. When you affirm, compliment, or support a friend, your relationship grows stronger, but when you reject, criticize, or tear down a friend, your relationship weakens. If the relationship incurs too many negative interactions, the friendship risks falling apart and terminating.

A friendship, like a human life, is a dynamic affair, and the only constant in this endeavor is change. Friendships require nurturing and investment. Do you reach out to your friends as much as they do to you? An important social skill that supports longevity in friendships is initiation. Do you take initiative and reach out to friends, or do they mainly reach out to you? What priority do you place on relationships? These considerations can determine how long friendships will last in your life.

Some people are born networkers; it comes naturally to them. They are the friends who get the group together for social activities and make phone calls or send emails to keep in touch. Do you know people like this? If these networkers within friendships did not exist, nobody would see each other. Whether you are a natural-born networker or not, we can learn from those who are. You can start by taking the initiative and randomly calling a friend. Random calls are becoming a lost art in our overscheduled digital age, but you don't need an appointment or an agenda to call a friend. Just reach out and say, "I was just thinking of you and hope you are doing well. Hope we can catch up soon."

ENDING A FRIENDSHIP

Not all friendships are destined to last. Sometimes, a friendship fades into a relationship that no longer provides much joy or solace. Friendship can be tested by actions or behaviors that undermine its foundation. How would you feel if you found out your best friend had stolen from you or lied to you or betrayed you? You might find it in your heart to forgive your friend, but you might also find it difficult to continue the friendship. The hard truth is that, sometimes, circumstances dictate ending a friendship.

The reality is that some friendships will simply wither away. Time passes, people move, and when efforts are not made to stay in touch, a mutual disconnect is implied. This occurrence tends to be more acceptable with acquaintances or activity buddies. Yet, with close friends, relationship termination warrants communication. As in any situation, you will want to check in with your values. Do you wish people well or ill when they depart? What if they have hurt you? Do you still wish them well?

Assuming you wish people well, you may want to consider the following statements for ending a relationship:

- **"Be well, Frank. I have enjoyed knowing you, and maybe we will reconnect in the future."**
- **"You will always be in my thoughts and prayers, Frank."**
- **"I'm sorry we've had some disagreements, Frank, but I wish you well."**

The focus of these statements is either on the past relationship or the future outside of the relationship. However, all of these statements include a positive wish for the departing friend. The last statement acknowledges that there were some tough times in the relationship, but it closes in a positive manner. You can depart from this relationship in peace, and that is a huge benefit of a graceful termination.

CHAPTER 6

DATING

This chapter will focus on how to implement your social skills when dating. Dating can be a difficult social space to navigate because the stakes are high. It touches our human desire to connect with another person with a greater degree of intensity and on a different level than friendship. Friendship is a recommended goal of the dating process, but there is an additional goal of deeper emotional and physical intimacy. Like friendship, dating—and romantic love—involve vulnerability. Being vulnerable can be scary, but having strong social skills to rely on can give you more confidence.

GAUGING A POTENTIAL PARTNER'S INTEREST

Gauging the interest of a potential romantic partner is a tricky endeavor. We look for signals of attraction. We catch a smile. What did it mean? Was it simply a polite smile or something more? How we interpret the signals we think we're getting can be biased by our own interest. Are we seeing more than what's really there?

Humans are constantly interpreting communication from others and the world around them. Through this interpretation process, we weigh all the possible options and select what we believe to be the most probable message. Of course, this usually happens in an instant. But with dating, when the stakes are high and our desires are strong, we can end up ruminating on what we think the other person was conveying. Successfully reading cues during interactions with this person will go a long way toward determining if there's interest. Some people are exceptionally good at this, while others may need a bit more coaching. Regardless, anyone can get better at gauging interest by calling on their social skills.

Communication is not just about the content you want to convey but the emotional stage you want to set. If you are seeking to connect with a person for the purpose of dating, the emotional stage will be all the more important because dating relationships are heavily driven by emotions. Small talk and nonverbal communication are front and center when gauging the interest of a potential dating partner. Small talk gets the conversation going, sets the emotional stage, and puts the other party at ease.

FROM FRIENDSHIP TO THE FIRST DATE

In today's online dating world, the first date may be the initial connection, or a friendship may develop first, then evolve into a first date. Friendship is built on sharing something in common with another person. What do you have in common with the other person that you can build upon to create a relationship? Some of the same skills you used to gauge interest will be helpful here.

The move from friendship to the first date can happen in a number of ways. You may have known this friend for some time and would like to get closer by shifting to a dating relationship. The online dating format is targeted toward a specific goal, and the initial connection is primarily focused on discerning an appropriate fit for dating. Whether your friendship is combined with your dating inquiry or you've been friends for some time, there is a clear transitional moment when the relationship gets redefined as dating. This is a milestone moment, but it's important not to leave the friendship part of your relationship behind as the intensity ramps up.

With the shift from friendship to dating, there is a greater need for social skills that foster deeper connection. Listening and asking questions are critical skills during this stage when dating partners get to know each other in an accelerated fashion. Friends tend to spend less time together, so they have more to talk about when they do get together. Dating partners are together more, so their conversations can actually take more work since you may run out of things to say. Listening closely and deriving questions from what you've heard is essential to developing the connection. You are on a mission to build a relationship here, so if you want the relationship to last, it will require effort. It can be challenging but also immensely rewarding as you and your partner explore compatibility that may lead to a life partnership.

BUILDING A ROMANCE

Romance is a powerful force that drives excitement in the dating domain. Partners who are building their romance are highly motivated to please each other and spend lots of time together. Lovers are face-to-face, absorbed in their bond. Brain chemicals associated with pleasurable rewards flood their brains. This produces a variety of responses, including racing heartbeats, flushed cheeks, and feelings of passion. Everything outside of the relationship becomes secondary, and there is an exclusivity to the relationship that is highly comforting and soothing. But what is the path from first date dinner and a movie to full-blown romance? Which social skills in your toolbox can you use to help your budding relationship blossom? Romance is so powerful that it must be managed well. There are potential pitfalls along the way, which is why good social skills are necessary when building a romantic relationship.

Assertiveness is an important social skill to use during the romance phase. Through assertiveness, you can name your needs, especially around vulnerability and managing emotions. Romance can be filled with many misinterpretations. It's possible that your partner will have friends of the opposite sex, and you may be curious about or feel threatened by their relationship to those friends. Through the use of assertiveness, you can make your needs known to your partner, which gives them the opportunity to validate them. These sensitive conversations will build intimacy or help you learn whether or not this relationship is a good fit for you. Practicing assertiveness during the romance stage will set the tone for addressing difficult issues throughout the relationship.

MAINTAINING A HEALTHY CONNECTION

Romance is a wonderful part of a relationship, one to be savored and appreciated. Ultimately, though, to facilitate a long-term healthy connection, friendship must exist alongside romance. After the feel-good, neurochemical-driven, blind love phase of the relationship, the brain resets back to normal. At this time, friendship carries the weight of supporting the couple, and a common vision and values will have a major impact on the connection. A healthy connection is also maintained when a couple prioritizes common courtesy, compassion, and kindness. This is where communication and social skills come into play.

Character strengths also help with social skills. If you have strengths of humor and creativity, you can use these to initiate connection to your partner. If your partner has strength in leadership, then they can combine that with assertiveness to promote a common vision for your relationship. If one of your strengths is wisdom, then you can use that to assist with decision-making. Kindness is a character strength that aligns well with empathy. With this strength, a person can be helpful in many ways without expecting anything in return. Kindness is motivated by feelings of empathy and concern that expresses a genuine need. The interplay between values, strengths, and social skills is an important dynamic in maintaining a healthy connection. Couples counseling can be another valuable addition to this process that can help you fine-tune your connection and understand each other in a deeper way. Expectations will become more realistic, as you'll know how you complement your partner when facing the challenges of life.

MAKING IT LAST

A relationship must have a shared purpose for it to be sustainable. What is your relationship about? Even more important, where are each of you going? Are you headed in the same direction? Personality, attraction, and chemistry play key roles in beginning and maintaining a relationship, but none plays a primary role in making a relationship last for many years. Let's be honest: Over time, people can get on each other's nerves. When that happens, what will sustain you? The answer is shared interests, shared values, and the all-important common vision; these are all the things that keep people invested in a relationship over the long term. Common vision is especially important because a relationship must have purpose for it to be sustainable.

A common vision is built on shared values. If I value family life at home and my partner values travel, then we may have conflicting visions. If I value money and my partner values sacrifice, that may also create a conflicting vision. If I value spirituality and my partner values hedonism, once again, this might make the creation of a common vision somewhat challenging. While some common visions can be more challenging than others to create, they are essential to lasting relationships and require social skills.

Active listening and questions filled with genuine curiosity are necessary in building a common vision. Take your time with the process of vision building by trusting and practicing your social skills. Using social skills to effectively communicate your desires for a common vision can be difficult, but doing so in pieces can ease the pressure. Consider how long you can actively listen to your partner before getting distracted. Call this out upfront by saying, "Let's discuss our common vision for

30 minutes." Setting expectations based on your ability to use your social skills will avoid the letdown of failed interactions. Creating something in common is what communication is all about. The social skills used during this difficult process will pay off in the end with a strong common vision that you and your partner will look to for a sustaining relationship long past the romance phase.

MEETING FAMILY AND FRIENDS

The prospect of meeting your partner's family and friends can produce anxiety. Questions about the encounter include: Will I be judged or welcomed? Will I appear awkward or competent? Will I say something inappropriate or come across as interesting and thoughtful? The approval of your partner's family and friends is no small matter. Implementing social skills under stress adds another layer to the challenge. Using techniques to manage stress, like breathing and exercise, will also be important in directing your energy to present well instead of recoiling in fear.

Open-ended questions will be important when meeting your partner's family and friends. Questions that relate to your partner and their background are especially relevant here. In addition, be on the lookout for common interests that you may share with this new group of people, as well. Remember how friendships are built on shared interests? Your big shared interest with your partner's friends is your partner! Creative inquiries promote the exploration of common interests. And if you get stuck or can't think of a question to ask, you can paraphrase or repeat back what a particular person has said. This is a handy tool for encouraging people to talk more. For example, consider the following dialogue that uses paraphrasing:

You: So, you all moved out to California from New Jersey?
Partner's parent: Yes, it was a big move when Sally was 12.

You: Sally was 12?
Partner's parent: Yes. I know that's a tough age to move, but we really had no choice.

You: Twelve is a tough age . . . It's the beginning of adolescence.
Partner's parent: Yes, but she made some new friends fairly quickly.

You: I could see that. She is very likeable.
Partner's parent: I think she gets that from her mother!

The conversation will likely continue with an equal balance of back and forth. You can see active listening with paraphrasing and repeating moves the conversation along quite nicely. In this instance, you won't need to think of new material all that much. It's also topic of an appealing shared interest. What parent doesn't like to talk about their child? Using these skills, along with stress and anxiety management, will set you up for success when meeting your partner's family and friends.

CHAPTER 7

WORKPLACE INTERACTIONS

The workplace is a critical domain of our lives that requires effective social skills. Coworker, client, and manager relationships all require careful social navigation. Ample research highlights the importance of emotional intelligence (EQ) in the workplace. Depending on your career, emotional intelligence can have a greater impact on your success than your knowledge (IQ). Your IQ may get you a job, but a lack of EQ can get you fired. Dr. Travis Bradberry reported that emotional intelligence is responsible for 58 percent of success on the job, and 90 percent of top performers have high EQ.

The benefits of emotional intelligence on the job are many. You will reap the rewards of a friendly environment and social nurturing at your workplace. Human decision-making has a significant emotional component, so others will more likely include you in special team projects and advancement opportunities if you bring high emotional intelligence to the workplace. Working on a team that is high functioning increases the likelihood of success. Emotional intelligence enables you to function optimally, and it is an important part of your social skills toolbox in the workplace.

THE INTERVIEW

An employment interview is where a first impression happens. What makes a good first impression? Image plays a role, so how you dress is important. You want to put your best foot forward, and the key will be exercising good social skills. You will almost certainly engage in small talk before the formal interview begins. This sets the stage and tone for the interview experience. A statement of gratitude is always a good topic for small talk, such as, "Thank you for seeing me today. I'm looking forward to learning more about this position." And of course, common topics like the weather or inquiries around general well-being are appropriate for small talk.

As the interview gets underway and you go about answering the interviewer's questions, keep in mind not only the content of your answers but the way you deliver them. Does your voice sound strong and self-assured? All the nonverbal topics discussed previously will be important to attend to in an interview. Is your body posture upright and attentive yet relaxed and confident? How is your eye contact? The most important skill of all in an interview is being aware of your audience. What do you notice about the person or people who are interviewing you? Are they distracted or engaged? This is a lot to think about, but as you get better at social skills, these skills will become second nature to you.

If it is difficult for you to get a sense of whether the interviewer likes or dislikes your answers, don't hesitate to ask. Questions or statements can be helpful to ensure you are on the right track with your interview.

1. Are my answers aligned with what you are looking for?

2. Is my answer relevant to the job requirements?

3. Please let me know if I'm going too fast or slow with my answers.

In most cases, you will not need to ask these questions, but they do show that you care about the interviewer and how they are receiving your answers. This is all in the service of getting a good read on your audience, the interviewer.

PRESENTATION TIME

Presentations can be made to one person or a group of people. You may be addressing your coworkers, your manager, or the company CEO. The presentation may be made in an office, a conference room, or a large hall. No matter the size of your audience, who your audience is, or the setting, as the presenter, you are in the spotlight, and being in the spotlight can be anxiety-producing. How do you overcome your anxiety and calm your nerves? Having confidence in your social skills is a great place to start.

Confidence is obtained in a number of ways, but the most important way is through experience. Practice your social skills as much as you can. Look for low-stakes situations where you can deliver presentations. Try using one of the following circumstances to prepare:

- **Gather friends and family for a dry run of your presentation.**
- **At a group meeting, raise your hand and make a relevant comment of support or praise.**
- **Set a goal to ask one or two questions in a classroom setting.**

Anytime you speak in situations where multiple people are listening is an opportunity to practice social skills that will help when giving presentations. Every opportunity to use social skills in a presentation will strengthen your confidence for the real presentation.

Confidence in your social skills during a presentation shows up in several ways. The first is your voice. If you are in a large room, will the people in the back be able to hear you? Are you speaking clearly, and do your sentences end definitively? Are your ideas being delivered in a digestible way to your audience? Posture and body position are other important social skills. Do you present as hunched over or upright and confident? Do you face away from the audience or toward them, inviting a connection? Eye contact is also central to exuding confidence while using social skills. Pick a person to make eye contact with for a brief time as you are talking. You can also pick a spot in the room to look at if it is hard for you to look people in the eye. Just be careful to avoid an empty spot in the room where nobody is present.

BUSINESS MEETING

Business meetings involve speaking to a group of people while also practicing good listening skills. Business meetings usually have an agenda and goals. Tensions can rise in meetings when there are disagreements. Remaining detached when emotions escalate is not easy. How do you react when people disagree with you? Being able to manage your ego to the point where you are not attached to being right is part of emotional intelligence and good social skills. Another reason for conflict in meetings is misinterpretation. Multiple people are listening to each other, and each person may interpret what is said differently. The key to success here is to be very observant. After you speak, is your message acknowledged in a verbal or nonverbal way, or does the conversation veer off in a different direction? Does anyone ask you, directly or indirectly, to expand on your comments?

Active listening is extremely important during business meetings. Not only can this skill minimize misinterpretations, it can also help you manage your emotions. When someone disagrees with your point of view, you may feel anger escalating toward that person. In this situation, the immediate step is to de-escalate by being calm and reasonable. Paraphrasing or repeating what was recently said is a very effective way to achieve this and serves two purposes:

1. It validates the other person in a way that says, "I respect what you said by letting you know I heard it correctly."

2. It provides you with time to calm your emotions and reconnect to your "thinking brain." Our reactive emotional brain fires into action much quicker than our thinking, logical brain.

Active listening can help validate the other person's thoughts and manage your emotions so you appear cool, collected, and reasonable in a business meeting. If you happen to disagree with a point of view, do so in a measured, thoughtful way.

Another challenging part of a business meeting is speaking. Different personality types experience different challenges with being vocal. Extroverts will have an easier time jumping into a group conversation than introverts. Introverts tend to rehearse what they want to say before saying it out loud but have a harder time initiating speaking, so their comments are typically more succinct. Knowing your personality type will help you use the appropriate social skills necessary to find the right balance when you participate in business meetings.

HOLIDAY GATHERING

Holiday gatherings occur in both personal and professional domains. These gatherings require a significant amount of small talk, which can be the hardest part of a work-related holiday gathering, especially if you attend it by yourself.

You walk into a room filled mostly with people you barely know. You scan the room looking for familiar faces. Maybe you find one—but maybe you don't. Does your anxiety rise? Are you tempted to leave? Social gatherings are the most challenging social situations you'll have to deal with. Why? Because there is no clearly defined goal except to be social! Small talk may lead to a topic of interest, but the conversation may just flounder and fizzle out. These are hard situations to manage if you are self-conscious about your social skills. The three key social skills to master for all social gatherings are greetings, questions and listening, and exits.

Greetings begin with eye contact. Imagine walking around a gathering or sitting at a table with a group of people. The first thing that happens is eye contact with other guests, and this action is often followed by a smile. This interaction sets the emotional tone. You can then continue with a clear greeting that could be as simple as "Hi, I'm Frank." After the initial greeting, questions are critical for success. Good questions come from active listening skills. General or vague questions usually don't interest people much. Listen to what the other person is saying and try to formulate a relevant question to keep their interest. This back-and-forth banter can keep the conversation going for some time. You will also get a sense of how talkative the other party is and how much effort you will need to put into the conversation. Eventually, it will be time to exit the conversation. Exit statements can be things like "Good to chat with you" or "I better get going now." You can also use nonverbal movements, such as stepping back, to indicate an exit. This combined with an exit statement is usually the best.

Be gentle with yourself. Holiday gatherings are a challenge. Do not feel like you have to stay for hours or until the gathering closes. Set small goals for yourself. Maybe you can strive for one or two good conversations, and then leave. Increase your goals for the next social gathering. Over time, your confidence will increase as your skills improve.

CUSTOMER/CLIENT SERVICE

Interacting with customers or clients may or may not be central to your job. Either way, the stakes tend to be high when customers are involved. Customers are the source of revenue and ultimately the reason that your workplace exists in the first place. If you are self-employed, then your customers are your bosses. We live in an age where customer success is paramount. How can you be effective with your new social skills in such a high-pressure situation? What is the best way to handle difficult-to-please customers and clients?

The first task is to acknowledge that this is a professional, not a personal social interaction. This changes everything. For example, during my work as a therapist, I tell my patients that they cannot offend me. They should be comfortable enough to relax, experiment, and present however they feel. Our time is about their growth and development. I simply smile and ask that my patients help me understand what they mean by their statements. This is very freeing for people, and it is for me, too. I do not take anything personally because I know the setting is professional, not personal.

The central social skills needed succeed in this professional framework are active listening and empathy. The customer first needs to know and feel like you care. Without that sense of care and concern, the interaction is headed for trouble. We show that we care through active listening and empathy. Statements like "I'm sorry our product didn't meet your expectations" and "It sounds like our product did not resolve your problem" can go a long way in making an interaction positive. This does not mean that you cannot be direct and say, "Unfortunately your product is out of warranty at this time." The important thing to remember is to lead with bad news and, if you can, follow up with alternative solutions. An example of this might be, "The product is out of warranty, but there may be some repair options we can explore."

Customer service is conducted via voice, email, and online chat. Each of these modalities has its strengths and weaknesses. Familiarize yourself with your modality, acknowledge your professional setting, and use your social skills of active listening and empathy to ensure the customer is heard and validated. This will make difficult statements, like "The product is out of warranty," much easier to convey.

LUNCHTIME CHATTER

The workplace cafeteria or break room is generally a relaxed setting where hungry people gather for a meal or snack. Because people like to eat, lunchtime puts them in a good mood, so the atmosphere is usually light and upbeat. This sets the stage for some casual social interactions. Conversations are easy to start with simple remarks, like "What's for lunch?" or "How's the soup today?" One of the nice aspects of any meal is that people go back and forth between focusing on their food and the people they're with. This means that the pressure of keeping a conversation constantly moving is removed. Of course, there are some basic rules when interacting socially around food—like don't talk with your mouth full. But what other guidelines are there for a casual meal in a work environment, and what social skills are most in play?

Due to the relaxed, informal nature of lunchtime chatter, our old friend, small talk, surfaces as an essential social skill. Food is the focus of lunch as opposed to an agenda-driven business meeting. The only reason people are chattering over food is because most people find it fun to socialize while eating. Asking open-ended questions can facilitate small talk. Topics can be work related or personal. Appropriate topics will be determined by the type of relationship you have with your lunch mates.

Personality styles also play a role here. Introverts may prefer to focus on the tasty bowl of soup and not be bothered with chatter. Extroverts may chew quickly so they can get back to the conversation. Notice your inclination during lunchtime. What is easy for you to do, and where do you notice resistance? Reflect on your wants and needs;

many times, they are different. You may want people to leave you alone so you can enjoy your soup, but you also may want social interaction. Do not be afraid to challenge yourself and discover what feels appropriate for you, then employ your social skills to achieve that balance. We need to be nourished in both ways—through nutrition and social connection. Lunchtime chatter offers a unique opportunity to do both.

CHAPTER 8

GROUP AND PUBLIC SETTINGS

Group and public settings can be challenging because initiating or jumping into a conversation can be difficult. On the other hand, these settings can also be easier because you don't have to talk all the time. Multiple people can share the talking load, so it takes the pressure off each person. This is especially beneficial if you are an introvert. You can be silent when you want to be and speak up when you choose. Social skills outside of personal settings, where you know everyone, and professional settings, where it is part of your job to be there, are of critical importance. Relationships change, and new people surface in our lives. A full life involves being open to new relationships. The social skills we use with someone we have just met are important because this new person could be your future best friend or spouse or business partner.

JOINING IN A GROUP

The attitudes and values of those already communicating in a group can make joining the conversation either simple or more difficult. If the group is friendly and values welcoming new people, entering the conversation will be much easier. If the group is exclusive and appears closed off, entry will be more of a challenge. It is a nice gift when a group of people pause to acknowledge a newcomer and welcome them into their conversation. Nonverbal social skills are needed to support entry into a group conversation in progress.

Consider what type of presence you offer when approaching the group. Do you have adequate eye contact, or are you looking away? Is your facial expression welcoming and engaging or negative and off-putting? Are you facing the group or more tentative in your posture or stance? Do you appear relaxed or nervous? Monitoring and being self-aware of your nonverbal social cues will help as you present yourself and join in a group conversation.

Open-ended questions are another social skill that is valuable when joining a group conversation. You will want to find out what people are discussing so you're able to participate in the conversation, as well. You may have overheard bits and pieces of the conversation but are not aware of all the details. You could say, "I heard you guys talking about the Badgers. I've been following them all year. They are having quite a season!" You could also combine open-ended questions with an introduction: "Hi, I'm Frank. How is everyone doing today?"

Combining effective nonverbal skills with open-ended questions will help you join group conversations in a variety of settings. Like many other social tasks, it is better to join more laid-back conversations than those that appear more animated. Also, a conversation among family members will likely be easier to join than a conversation among coworkers you do not know at a work function. Set your expectations and goals appropriately and challenge yourself at an incremental pace.

MAKING A GROUP OF FRIENDS

When people come together over a shared interest, connections are bound to be made. A connection over a strong shared interest can develop into a friendship. When several people bond over a shared interest and forge friendships, the result is a group of friends. It is unlikely that each member of the group will have an equally strong bond with every other member, as many factors figure into the creation of friendships. For instance, personality type is a big factor that can impact friendships. If you're an introvert, you may not feel as connected to the talkative, outgoing extroverts in the group as you do to the other introverts. A group of friends adds a whole other dimension to the notion of friendship, but developing a group of friends presents its own social skills challenges.

Social bonds over common interests can be powerful for the members and for the goals of a group. Social activists are more effective when they gather in groups. Friends who love a sport will be more excited and motivated to interact because of the social connection. The social motivator is one of the most powerful forces we know of to create good habits. Every group of friends needs a networker or organizer. Who steps up and reaches out to make things happen? Is that you, or do you prefer to be a follower? This networking role can be shared, but what are the social skills needed to function as an organizer of a group of friends?

Assertiveness is the social skill needed to make a group of friends. This means you have the courage and sensitivity to contact others and motivate them to connect in ways that are welcoming and inviting. This might mean emailing an invitation to go cycling on Saturday or reaching out to say hello to a member of the group. At some point, someone must take action for the group friendships to build and develop. Taking action and being assertive require energy. This energy is well spent when the social connection occurs. Group bonding happens, and shared experiences are created. Many of our greatest memories are of shared gatherings of friends. Are you acting in assertive ways to reach out and do the networking needed to build and sustain your group of friends?

HOSTING A PRIVATE EVENT

Hosting a private event can be a small or large undertaking. When you host a private event, you are the greeter who welcomes people and the organizer who explains what is going to happen. These roles require significant social energy, as you want everyone to enjoy the event. Making sure everything goes as planned is one priority, and connecting with people at the event is another; one task is more managerial, while the other is more social. Hosting an event requires a focus that is very different from just showing up and being social, and hosting can actually lighten the load of needing to be "socially on" all the time. For instance, you can move in and out of groups without struggling to find ways to leave a conversation. Everyone knows you have a lot happening, and they don't expect you to linger long. Whether you have the gift of hospitality or need to work at it, what social skills are most useful when hosting a private event?

Once again, assertiveness is a central social skill needed when hosting a private event. Because of your dual roles of socializing and running the event, you will have to balance your time effectively. You may have to enter or exit conversations quickly because of a sudden need that surfaces. Maybe the caterer is running late or someone is leaving and wants to offer their farewell. Maybe you need something from another person and have to step in and pull them away from their conversation. Assertiveness is essential in all of these cases, and it enables you to get your task done without being aggressive. You can use phrases like "Please excuse me" and "I'm sorry to interrupt, but . . ." and "Let's pick up later. I need to check on the lasagna."

Assertiveness is a verbal and nonverbal activity. You first need to get the other person's attention. Putting a hand on their shoulder or waving at them are effective nonverbal strategies to do this. You need to present with a clear, strong voice when being assertive: "Excuse me, Frank. Can I grab you for a minute?" Hosting a private event is not for everyone, but it can be very fun for those who enjoy hospitality and managing a lot of activities at once in a social setting.

CONFERENCES

Conferences take place in public settings with lots of people gathering to learn and network. Conferences offer a great opportunity to connect with other people and get new ideas. However, there is a hustle and bustle to a conference that can make the experience feel chaotic. If you get overwhelmed in a chaotic environment, it's a good idea to spend some time before the conference reviewing the agenda and setting a plan for your participation. You may need to interact with work colleagues or clients at the conference; at these times, you'll need to be your most lively and engaged. After a conference is over, there is usually a follow-up period. Who did you meet at the conference? What is the potential for the interaction to continue in a meaningful way? As you can tell, a variety of social skills is required during and after a conference.

A combination of small talk, questions, and assertiveness is needed for an experience at a conference to go well. Small talk will help because conferences are significant networking opportunities. You may be seated at a lunch table with people you've never met, or you may be in a breakout session with people who share a common interest. These are all opportunities for you to connect and network. With all these potential new connections available, conferences present a short but intense social setting filled with opportunities. Small talk begins the connection, and then questions deepen the interaction. Geographic inquiries and statements are great for starting a conversation: "Where did you travel from?" or "They sure picked a beautiful setting for this conference."

Assertiveness will also be required at conferences because people are moving around a lot. They move from breakout sessions to vendor booths to lunch venues. Seating may be limited, or you may prefer a better seat up front and must arrive early. Those are the practical aspects of assertiveness at a conference. Initiating conversation during and after the conference also requires assertiveness. You may meet someone you think can help you get a better job or a contractor you would like to consider hiring. Think of salespeople at conferences. Their job is to be assertive during and after the conference. While you may not be selling anything, you are seeking to initiate or follow up on a social connection. Assertiveness will help you accomplish this during and after a conference.

SPORTS ACTIVITIES

Sports activities provide an ideal opportunity to use our social skills. The activities draw together motivated people with a shared interest, creating the perfect climate for connections to be made and friendships to develop. Sports activities usually involve competition and teamwork. The urge to compete and the desire to win provide participants with something to rally around and talk about. Sports activities often involve lots of movement, and emotions improve with movement. As emotions improve, anxiety is reduced, and endorphins are released. Endorphins are an opioid produced by the body that make us feel good. When you feel good, you are more likely to reach out to others. When you are engaged in a sports activity, notice how easily the social interactions flow. At some point, you don't even have to think about them. It's the *flow state* that you are striving for. In these moments, you are using your social skills without any effort. Like athletes who get in the athletic zone when they are playing a sport, you can also get in the social zone when connecting with others during a sports activity.

There are many nonverbal social skills used during sports activities, but note that nonverbal is used loosely here. Sports activities involve fast-paced emotional moments that are constantly changing. One moment, the team scores a goal, and the next moment, someone strikes out. Most goals and successes are followed up by nonverbal interactions such as high fives, hugs, and shouts of victory. These are not well-thought-out, complete sentences but rather emotional responses to victory or, in some cases, defeat. Defeat is part of competing, and we must be prepared for that, as well. Putting your hand on your teammate's shoulder as their head hangs low after failing to come through in a clutch moment in the game is an example of a nonverbal interaction in a time of defeat.

Assertiveness is also an important part of a sports activity. Whether you are pleading with the coach to put you in the game or yelling at your teammate to pass the ball, assertiveness is necessary. Any competition requires assertiveness because you are trying to win. This could mean running faster than your opponent or outsmarting them on the field. Either way, you must assert yourself in a sports activity to compete.

A CAFÉ

A café is a fun public place to use your social skills. The random interactions that occur in public spaces are spontaneous and offer the opportunity to meet someone completely new. For example, say you're in an almost-empty café. You make eye contact with one of the few other customers. Maybe there is a smile, and then an urge to say hello. A witty comment or a remark about a current news matter may seem appropriate If the other person responds, an enjoyable conversation may follow. At some point, you may realize that the interaction is derailing your plans to get some work done. You then have a decision to make. How much of a priority is it for you to meet new people? Sometimes, your personal agenda needs to be put on hold so you can engage in positive social interactions. Social interactions feed us in ways that completing a solitary project cannot. Humans are fundamentally social creatures. When we don't get our fill of social interactions, we feel lonely and empty. Cafés offer opportunities for spontaneous social interactions that can feed us socially. Self-awareness is necessary in order to recognize when you are socially depleted or when you are socially satisfied and can focus on your work projects.

Small talk is a helpful skill when meeting new people at cafés. Usually, an initial comment surfaces that will engage the other person. This could be about the weather or current events, or it may even be a light compliment. It is important to present an inviting tone and to speak with confidence so that your message reaches its intended listener.

Listening is an important skill when interacting with people you know at cafés. Cafés can be busy places with lots of distractions. This can provide a welcome background for work in the form of white noise. But if you are trying to have a conversation, these distractions can make listening difficult. Active listening ensures that you heard what the other person has said. You can repeat or paraphrase their statements to ensure that you are both on the same page. At that point, you are well positioned to offer your thoughts on the topic and continue the conversation with an active, energetic café environment as a backdrop to your social interaction.

NOT THE FINAL WORD

We have discussed many topics in this book to support social skills. I congratulate you for investing your time and energy developing these crucial skills. Relationships are one of the most important ingredients of well-being. When people look back on their lives, they rarely wish they had spent more time in the office or had worked harder, but they do wish they had expressed their feelings more and had more contact with friends. It's relationships that matter the most as we move forward in life.

Part of nurturing relationships is expressing feelings and spending time with other people. It's quite the paradox that relationships are seen as so important when we look back on our lives, but when we're looking forward, we tend to discount them and favor spending our time on achievements and rewards. We all get one life, and we each get to choose how we spend our time. By building your social skills, you've taken a big step toward living a life you can look back on and be at peace with, knowing you did your best to nurture your relationships.

Social skills development is more than a matter of knowledge acquisition. You've done good work reading this book and pondering the ideas. You now have the tools to initiate and participate in conversations in many different settings. Yet even with the right tools, social situations can be intimidating. Like many things in life, using social skills gets easier with practice. You'll have breakthrough moments that surprise you and make gradual progress that affirms your efforts. Start with safe settings to take risks. Build your confidence little by little to increase your level of comfort in social settings. The payoff will be significant. Just like learning to play a musical instrument, for a while, it may seem like you're not making progress, but when the breakthrough moments come, you'll experience a strong sense of accomplishment and a big boost to your confidence.

Perseverance is critical, as you must expect failure from time to time. Don't be afraid to fail. Have fun and stay positive, especially after failures. That's where the major growth occurs on your road to using everyday social skills to experience the joy of the interpersonal human experience.

REFERENCES

American Psychiatric Association (APA). *Diagnostic and Statistical Manual of Mental Disorders*: DSM-5, 5th edition. Arlington, VA: American Psychiatric Association, 2017.

Anxiety and Depression Association of America (ADAA). "Anxiety and Depression." Accessed March 2020. adaa.org/about-adaa /press-room/facts-statistics.

Boyes, Alice. "4 Social Tips for Introverts." *Psychology Today*. Accessed March 2020. psychologytoday.com/us/blog/in-practice/201302/4 -social-tips-introverts.

Bradberry, Travis. "The Massive Benefits of Boosting Your Emotional Intelligence." World Economic Forum. Accessed March 2020. weforum.org/agenda/2020/02/emotional-intelligence-career -life-personal-development.

Davis, Tchiki. "What Is Self-Awareness, and How Do You Get It?" Accessed March 2020. *Psychology Today*. Posted March 11, 2019. psychologytoday.com/us/blog/click-here-happiness/201903/what -is-self-awareness-and -how-do-you-get-it.

Ekman, Paul. "Darwin's Contributions to Our Understanding of Emotional Expressions." *Philosophical transactions of the Royal Society of London. Series B, Biological Sciences,* vol. 364,1535: 3449-51. doi:10.1098/rstb.2009.0189, 2009.

Engel, Beverly. "Healing Your Shame and Guilt Through Self-Forgiveness." *Psychology Today*. Posted June 1, 2017. psychologytoday.com/us/blog /the-compassion-chronicles/201706/healing-your-shame-and-guilt -through-self-forgiveness.

MacGill, Markus. "What Is the Link between Love and Oxytocin?" Medical News Today. Accessed March 2020. medicalnewstoday.com /articles/275795#the_love_hormone.

Mayo Clinic. "Healthy Body Image: Tips for Guiding Girls." Accessed April 9, 2020. mayoclinic.org/healthy-lifestyle/tween-and-teen-health/in-depth/healthy-body-image/art-20044668.

Mehrabian, Alfred. *Silent Messages: Implicit Communication of Emotions and Attitudes.* Belmont: Wadsworth, 1981.

Seligman, Martin E. P. *Flourish: A Visionary New Understanding of Happiness and Well-being.* New York: Atria, 2012.

Tierney, John, and Roy F. Baumeister. "For the New Year, Say No to Negativity." *The Wall Street Journal.* Accessed March 2020. wsj.com/articles/for-the-new-year-say-no-to-negativity-11577464413.

Wang, D., and H. Li. *Nonverbal Language in Cross-Cultural Communication.* US-China Foreign Language, 2007.

Yamada, Kobi, and Steve Potter. *Ever Wonder: Ask Questions and Live into the Answers.* Lynnwood, WA: Compendium Pub, 2001.

INDEX

ABOUT THE AUTHOR

 **Dr. Thomas Lucking** is the founder and director of Silicon Valley Therapy and a professor of a master's-level psychology program. His practice provides psychotherapy, coaching, and consulting services to clients in the San Francisco Bay Area and beyond. He has received degrees in computer science, counseling psychology, theology, and completed his doctoral research in positive psychology. He has also created multiple therapeutic and coaching modalities including 167 Therapy, RMT (Relationship-based, Metric-driven Therapy), ISM (Island of Shared Meaning healthy communication), and waVe (With A Vision We All Excel).

He empowers individuals, couples, families, and teams by way of education, experiences, neurofeedback, and practical tools. This empowerment drives coherent communication, prosocial behavior, habit change, deep insights, reconciliation of past wounds, and relationships that thrive.

You can contact Dr. Lucking at ThomasLucking.com.

CPSIA information can be obtained
at www.ICGtesting.com
Printed in the USA
JSHW021236031020
8349JS00001B/1

9 781647 396442